THE ARMAGEDDON EXPERIENCE

THE ARMAGEDDON EXPERIENCE

—A Nuclear Weapons Test Memoir—

ROD BUNTZEN

Library of Congress Control Number:		2019900717
ISBN:	Hardcover	978-1-7960-1159-3
	Softcover	978-1-7960-1158-6
	eBook	978-1-7960-1157-9

The Armageddon Experience, Front Cover Image:
Title: Operation Hardtack I OAK/8.9 Megatons/Enewetak Atoll/1958
Credit Line: © 2003 Michael Light 100 Suns

The Armageddon Experience, Back Cover Image.
Title: Sather Gate, University of California, Berkeley, California
Author photo, 1/12/2019

Print information available on the last page.

Rev. date: 02/13/2019

To order additional copies of this book, contact:
Xlibris
1-888-795-4274
www.Xlibris.com
Orders@Xlibris.com
786423

When the last witness to nuclear Armageddon is gone,
The temptation to create others will become irresistible.

Rod Buntzen

CONTENTS

PREFACE

A chilling echo of the nuclear fear permeating America's public during the Cold War with the Soviet Union is growing louder today, with new reports about North Korea's progress on atomic weapons and long-range missiles, Iran's desire for similar technologies, and Russia's and China's increasing pushback against the U.S. role in the world. In addition, uncontrollable Middle East violence and hatred of the U.S. is contributing to the possibility that nuclear weapons may someday detonate on American soil. Unfortunately, few of our leaders remember the horror that nuclear weapons can cause, and the public today has little understanding of what was at stake during the Cold War and what to expect from a nuclear explosion in one of our cities.

The Armageddon Experience recounts my experience as an undergraduate science student working at a little-known, top-secret Navy laboratory in the San Francisco Bay Area, preparing for nuclear weapon tests in the Pacific. It tells of my journey from the 1950s University of California, Berkeley to the Pacific Proving Grounds— from campus life to secret national defense research and interactions with Manhattan Project scientists. The possibility of a dangerous political decision or an accident during the Cold War created a climate of existential fear that loomed over all those involved.

I describe how I came to stand on the beach of a far-away Pacific island, barely outside the safe zone, to experience a multi-megaton nuclear Armageddon unfolding second-by-second before me. In addition to descriptions of the science and phenomenology of such horror, I relate the staggering impact the open-atmosphere nuclear tests had on native Enewetak and Bikini Atoll populations, as well as on Japanese fishermen caught by "the sun that rose in the west." What my colleagues and I experienced affected our lives and threatened the future existence of our nation. Both curious and cautious at the time, I projected the physical and radiation damage I had come to understand from such a detonation onto the San Francisco Bay Area and describe the escape route I would take if a situation like the Cuban Missile Crisis were to continue to heat up.

My Armageddon experience was Operation Hardtack I, Shot *Oak*, witnessed from a distance of just twenty miles. Although not the horror the victims of Hiroshima and Nagasaki experienced, *Oak's* yield was 500 times greater and portended a proportional nightmare, if ever deployed. Operation Hardtack I consisted of 35 nuclear detonations at the Bikini, Enewetak, and Johnston atolls between April 28 and August 18, 1958. Hardtack II followed Hardtack I later that year at the Nevada Test Site (now the Nevada National Security Site), consisting of another 37 much lower yield detonations.

The Hardtack I and II tests took place near the end of the U.S. open-atmosphere nuclear weapons testing program that began with Operation Crossroads in 1946. Following Hardtack I and II, the U.S. unilaterally agreed to a testing moratorium that held for three years, until broken when the Soviets began testing again in 1961. The U.S. responded the next year with Operation Dominic. Finally, the U.S and Soviet Union signed a multi-country Limited Test Ban Treaty in Moscow in 1963, although the Soviet Union, as well as several other countries, continued open-atmosphere testing until 1980. Nuclear weapon technology has spread and is now a major international concern, even though the U.S. and Russia significantly reduced their stockpiles after the Cold War.

While military and terrorist threats abound in the early 21st century, the true Armageddon experience faced by the people in Hiroshima and Nagasaki is no longer discussed. Those of us who have witnessed the detonation of a multi-megaton nuclear weapon are an aging population and few (if any) are now involved in American defense policy and strategic planning. Nuclear disarmament has never been a popular topic in U.S. political discourse, and today we are planning to modernize our remaining warheads. Unfortunately, little of the widespread existential fear for our survival that these weapons generated during the Cold War remains to contribute to the debate facing our leaders.

I have included information and activities from before, during, and after my experience in Hardtack I to help relate the personal side of the unique work my colleagues and I pursued and to highlight some of the issues the public discussed during that period in our nation's history. In addition, this memoir contributes to the unrecorded history of the unique research carried out by a small, highly focused, top-secret Navy laboratory during the Cold War.

ACKNOWLEDGMENTS

Constructing this memoir after so many years was challenging, since I had kept only a partial diary of my daily activities while on Enewetak Atoll in the Pacific Proving Grounds. Fortunately, that diary provided descriptions of major events I experienced and added detail to what I could pull from memory about personal interactions with colleagues. Many day-to-day activities and personal interactions with colleagues taking place between nuclear detonations are, unfortunately, lost.

I thank Bob Hammond, Glynn Pence, Walt Gurney, Roger Caputi, Lou Gomez, Tak Shirasawa, Paul Zigman, and other Naval Radiological Defense Laboratory colleagues who helped me recall some of the events, problems, and good times we shared. I give special thanks to my boss, Evan Cyfeiliog Evans III, for his contributions. I look forward to when we next meet for lunch and talk about our times together.

I have taken liberties with descriptive dialog to relate some of the experiences that I cannot perfectly remember in order to convey the excitement and intense emotion I felt at the time (which I do remember). Key Wikipedia and other web sources are included to augment my memory regarding geographic areas and objects I describe in the text. Subjective comments and interpretations of events are my own, as are any factual errors.

I thank my wife, Joan, for her research support and unending editing, without which the memoir would have been impossible. I also thank my family, relatives, and friends for their critical but helpful comments.

Parry Island, Enewetak Lagoon in the Northwest Pacific, 1930 hours (GMT), 28 June 1958.

"Ten seconds to detonation," the voice on the loudspeaker announced. "9, 8, 7, 6, 5, 4, 3, 2, 1, Fire!"

...

...

"JESUS, it's bright—and it's getting hot!" I exclaimed.

...

They must have made a mistake, I thought.
Oak is going over 10 megatons!
I should start counting so I can estimate the yield.
One thousand one.
One thousand two.
One thousand thr—
Damn, I didn't start soon enough. If I go beyond ten, what difference will it make? WE'LL ALL FRY!
Beginning to panic, I slowly turned sideways to expose a different side of my clothing to the fireball.

CHAPTER 1

Berkeley Days

I thought about it repeatedly all morning long. Finally, I could not contain my thoughts any longer and decided to ask Ron if he had seen the advertisement—the one for a summer job that morning in the *San Francisco Chronicle*.

"The one about the radiation laboratory?" he answered.

"Yes, the one in San Francisco."

"There's no radiation laboratory in San Francisco," Ron replied. "You mean the cyclotron lab on the hill?"

"No, I remember it mentioned the Navy," I responded. "Are you going to apply for it?"

He paused. "I don't know."

Ron Johnston and I were lounging about the living room of the Sigma Chi Fraternity House one spring afternoon in 1957. It must have been a tough year for me at the University of California, (Cal) Berkeley, because only an echo of that conversation (and most of that semester) remains for me today. I know I had a good time that year though because my grades were just above the C^+ average required to remain in the engineering-physics curriculum. I'm no genius, so I must have found time away from fraternity life to pound the books. Still, I worried continually about failing. The newly formed program required engineering classes as well as the usual science and language units required by the physics curriculum. I faced homework problem sets from both the engineering and physics departments that took me forever to complete. Somehow, I made it through the fall semester, and as the spring semester ended, I was still hanging on.

Ron's major was physics; he was one of my few fraternity brothers enrolled in a science curriculum. A year ahead of me, he was looking for a summer job as well. He had a good chance of getting the summer job we had seen in the *San Francisco Chronicle*.

He continued, "I didn't save the paper and don't remember the name of the laboratory. It had a long name."

That was enough for me and within moments, I looked up the name of the laboratory in the phone book. Later that day, I called the laboratory's personnel office and, within a couple of days, drove across the Bay Bridge, turned south on Highway 101, and took an off-ramp to Hunters Point. I was looking for a large grey concrete building called the Naval Radiological Defense Laboratory (NRDL).

I got lost in the tangle of streets that lay between the freeway and the bay. It reminded me of when I'd first arrived in Berkeley a year earlier and gotten lost. I had turned onto Ashby Avenue off the freeway, and somehow missed College Avenue, which would have taken me to the campus. It had been a long drive from Los Angeles to Berkeley, and I must have been dreaming about my new life and trying to navigate at the same time. Berkeley was already turning out to be far different from the Los Angeles area surrounding the University of Southern California (USC) where I'd started earlier that day. The narrow streets, close-spaced stately older homes, and all the dense foliage that surrounded them had captured my attention.

NRDL turned out to be a windowless, fortress-like building inside the Hunters Point Naval Shipyard's south gate (Fig. 1), which I approached by traveling through a seedy, scary, low-cost housing area. Warned later by colleagues to spend as little time as possible in the area just outside the south gate, I often listened for gunshots from the nearby hillside when approaching the guard shack. (Bruce Moyer, the personnel officer who met me inside the NRDL building, did not mention any of this at the time.) My colleagues eventually told me about problems the Navy was experiencing from the local citizens outside the gate.

After filling out application forms requiring my life history and work experience (which primarily consisted of last year's summer job for the Navy in San Diego), Bruce introduced me to Takeo (Tak) Shirasawa, an assistant to a person named Evan Cyfeiliog Evans III. Bruce continued and casually added that Evan ran a field test program, which involved studying the effects of underwater nuclear weapons. *Wow, weird name, exciting program*, I thought. Tak proceeded to interview me about my technical background for the job posted in the *Chronicle*. At the time, I barely understood there was a difference between nuclear fission and fusion reactions. I related my Navy summer job in San Diego to Tak, hoping that he was interested enough to give me the job.

While living with my parents that summer, I had found a job in a student-engineering program with the Navy at the North Island Air Station in San Diego. My work involved designing and overseeing the building of a test stand for aircraft accelerometers. Armed with new technical skills from lower-division math and physics college classes, I eagerly fell into designing a small metal cage containing a rotating arm upon which an accelerometer could attach. Using simple formulae, I calculated the acceleration it experienced as the RPM of the arm was changed. Completing the design and finding the special parts needed, I oversaw construction of the test stand in the Air Station's fabrication shop.

The day finally arrived for testing my invention. It was two days before I would return to Berkeley for fall classes and my boss and several engineers gathered to watch the unveiling. If it worked, my device would end up testing reworked accelerometers for some of the Navy carrier-based aircraft undergoing repairs. The pressure freaked me out.

Several of us wheeled my test stand containing the rotating arm with an accelerometer over to its designated position, and the worker assigned to run tests looked about for a receptacle to plug it in. No 220-volt outlet! We quickly moved the test stand to a suitable outlet, and the motor to rotate the arm started. It seemed to work—for a while. The control meter faithfully indicated the arm's RPM, and the operator continued adjusting it using the control lever—again and again! Finally, he turned to my boss and said, "I can't adjust the RPM properly. The lever is too far away to watch the RPM dial and simultaneously make adjustments with my hand. I can't use this thing to calibrate accelerometers."

It turned out that he was farsighted and not able to see the meter when he had his hand on the control lever! I had placed the control lever low on the cage to simplify the linkage to the motor, which was perfectly okay for my arm length and eyesight, but not his. My boss said it was ok; they could make the proper changes. I left hoping that I would not need his recommendation for a future job.

The work Tak described to me at NRDL sounded exciting, and I guess I sounded acceptable to Tak. I would receive a temporary clearance, permitting access to secret material while the government conducted a background investigation of my life and character. I could start work after final exams.

I informed Ron that I had interviewed and gotten the NRDL job. At first, he appeared angry, and then he shrugged off the news and we returned to our friendly but distant relationship. We'd had a confrontation earlier in the spring in the parking lot next to the Sigma Chi house, and maybe I had jumped on the NRDL advertisement in retribution for his behavior. He had just been messing around, driving his car back and forth in the parking lot while I'd been polishing my newly acquired 1955 Austin Healey. While pulling up close, he'd managed to put a small mark on the Healey's rear fender. I'd been furious, and when he'd followed up on foot spouting some lip about my car, I'd hit him. He'd returned the punch. I'd ducked. We'd laughed, and it had been over, forgotten. However, I don't think he applied for other possible summer positions at NRDL after I told him I had been there first.

I needed a place to live during the summer since the lease on my shared apartment near campus was up. Venturing away from my comfortable Berkeley environment, I decided to live closer to my new work site and found a room in a small, modest apartment building in South San Francisco. The place was dreary but cheap and close to

NRDL. I worked long hours with my new colleagues, but the evenings were lonely and very different from my active fraternity life during the regular school year. I had long hours to think back about when I'd arrived in Berkeley, classes, and where my life might be heading.

The academic culture surrounding Cal dominated the city of Berkeley in the spring of 1956. A close relationship between the students and the neighborhood businesses existed that seems lost today. Telegraph Avenue, extending south toward Oakland from Cal's Sproul Plaza, today remains filled with small shops catering to students, but Shattuck Avenue, lying parallel a few blocks west, now holds a greatly expanded business center. In 1956, the Bank of America, on Telegraph Avenue, barely a block from the university's edge, had a glass-windowed façade facing the sidewalk instead of the current protective concrete block wall, built during the student demonstrations in the 60s.

The Cal student body, while culturally and spiritually mixed, was predominantly white and middle class and had fewer foreign students than it does today. Several overlapping cultures blended smoothly on campus to produce an idyllic college environment: a celebrated research and teaching faculty that included many Nobel Prize winners, a strong Greek fraternal organization, a contrasting but seemingly close-knit international student body, and a spirited and competitive sports following. When I arrived, Pat Brown was thinking about running for governor, Pappy Waldorf was the Golden Bears football coach, and Robert Gordon Sproul was Chancellor. Memorial Stadium, the Campanili, Earnest Lawrence's Cyclotron, and the Greek Theater stood in my mind as icons in competition with whatever the Ivy League schools could offer. What more could a young student ask for?

The "more" was to be found in the bohemian subculture that had spilled over from San Francisco and intersected but did not mix with Cal's student body. Its philosophy found basis in a European lifestyle that rejected materialism and pursued interests in eastern religions, alternative expressions of sexuality, and experimentation with drugs. Students attracted by this type of bohemianism and its Beat culture were ever-present in small groups around campus and individually in classrooms. They congregated in coffee shops and a couple of bookstores infrequently patronized by the other social groups on campus, and had favorite hangouts on both the north and south sides of campus. They stood in contrast to other student social groups. However, their lifestyle offered a curious and attractive alternative to fraternity life and, throughout my time at Cal, influenced me profoundly.

When I first arrived in Berkeley and found the Sigma Chi house, I immediately started the search for a roommate to share living costs. Since I was in good standing with my chapter at USC, it seemed that the Sigma Chi house was the logical place to begin the search for housing and roommates to help share the cost. I had spent the previous semester at USC living in the Sigma Chi house, and with tuition, room, and board being so expensive, I found that I had little money for social activities—not even for food on weekends when the fraternity kitchen provided a limited meal service. I remember mooching off my roommate some weekends in return for helping him make his way back to our room after extended drinking parties. Even though USC was fun, I couldn't afford it.

My plan at the time was to go to UC Berkeley for a period and possibly move on to the University of Washington. Although it had occurred to me to apply to an out-of-state school, I did not because Cal had accepted me into the engineering-physics curriculum for the 1956 spring semester. I was still feeling good about getting away from home after my first year in college at San Diego State College while living with my parents, and I grabbed the offer.

The newly formed engineering-physics program at Cal had courses from both the engineering and physics departments, to integrate both curriculums into a broader technical discipline. It offered a Bachelor of Science degree that eliminated some of the general education classes but demanded additional science units each semester to graduate. That was just what I wanted to pursue: a combination of both theoretical and practical technical classes. I later found there were only a dozen students in my graduating class and that a 2.5 grade point average was required to get a BS in engineering physics.

I had left Chula Vista High School with the intention of pursuing a career in music. Somehow, over the summer, I had decided to change my major from music to engineering. The reason for changing majors is a mystery to me still, but it appears to have originated from something that happened when Mr. Nichols, my science teacher, asked me to his house for hot apple cider and freshly made donuts during summer break. Looking back, I am grateful for Mr. Nichols' interest in me, and for possibly redirecting my career.

My rather beat up 1950 Mercury coupe sounded tired when I arrived in Berkeley, and I was relieved that I didn't have to push it further that day when I found the Sigma Chi house. I had sold my previous car earlier and, fortunately, one of my USC fraternity brothers was asking just $50 for the Merc. I entered the house and spotted a guy in his bathrobe sprawled out on a couch watching TV. Finding this behavior strange in the middle of the afternoon, I probably would not have approached him if there had been anyone else in sight. Classes were out between semesters and the house appeared empty.

The usual procedure for introducing one's self to someone you assumed might be another fraternity brother was first the "Hi, I'm Rod Buntzen, Delta Xi Chapter, San Diego State." If he responded in like manner, you'd extend the secret handshake to vet his membership. Bob Shugert responded appropriately and we began talking. He was recovering from a rather delicate male operation required by the Air Force ROTC before he could enter regular service, keeping him out of the day's normal activities. Hence, he was lounging about while everyone was away. He needed a place to live as well, and we quickly became friends.

Within days, we found a room to share in a house located half a block west, sloping down Channing Avenue from the Sigma Chi house toward the bay. The area now contains dorms and parking lots, but then Channing Avenue below College Avenue was a quiet street, lined with small houses, many of which had been converted into multiple apartments for students. I have long forgotten the address, but I remember that Bob and I shared a small room without a kitchen and relied on meals at the Sigma Chi house or hashing jobs for sustenance.

We felt fortunate that Joe Kapp and two other members of the Golden Bear's gridiron finest shared rooms in the same house. Their lifestyle was considerably different from ours, adding a bit of spice to our funds-limited existence by hosting parties and late-night activities.

Joe was about a couple inches over six feet tall and weighed in at a little over 200 pounds. He was quarterback for the Golden Bears from 1956 to 1958 when they took the PAC-8 championship and led them in their 1959 Rose Bowl attempt (12–38) against the Iowa State Hawkeyes. Joe possessed a good sense of humor and a laid-back, easygoing nature. Although we shared the Channing House together, Bob and I did not fit in with Joe's retinue of friends and attendants. One of the frequent visitors, Juan, was different from the others, and by chance, I got to know him a little better than Joe's other friends. He was a language tutor for the football team, sang opera, and often visited Joe and the others at the house for language tutoring sessions and some of the parties. Juan was gay, sensitive, and obviously out of place among the others, and I sensed the tension in him from Joe and his friends during his visits.

Joe went on to become a quarterback for professional Canadian and NFL teams and enjoyed a modest acting career. I remember seeing him in a movie on TV, *Climb an Angry Mountain*, in which he played an Indian fugitive whom Fess Parker's character tracked up Mt. Shasta. Joe and his outgoing housemates provided an exciting alternative to my daily routine during that first year at Cal.

Once Bob and I had settled into our small two-room and a bath suite, we searched for hashing jobs to provide a source of meals. I managed to get a job hashing at the Alpha Delta Pi sorority house, located on Channing Circle, while Bob returned to his earlier job hashing at the Delta Gamma sorority, just up Channing Avenue from the Sigma Chi house. They were sweet jobs, serving meals to the girls in return for food and a small stipend, which completely solved our sustenance problem.

Hashers' work started at lunchtime. We would bolt from classes when they ended at 11:50 a.m. to arrive at work at noon, don our stiffly starched white jackets, and set the tables appropriately for the food being prepared. Lunch was served at 12:15 p.m. Hands washed and hair combed, we carried plates containing lunch to the tables. Hashers would serve from the left while holding several plates lined up the free arm and held in place by the inoperative hand. My record, while keeping plate edges out of the mashed potatoes, was six plates. The Alpha Delta Pi house mother's place was at the end of the head table. We served her first, then the sorority officers sitting on each side of her. The remaining tables of girls chattered while waiting their turn.

Fraternity activities and difficult classes dominated my life. Fraternity chapter meetings and Friday afternoon social exchanges with sororities and the Merritt Nursing School won out over classes. Studying took low priority in comparison. Finals were always far away in the distant future.

The semester seemed to progress slowly that spring due to my social activities and the warm weather. It was destined to become a total loss unless I studied more and socialized less. I was trying to get serious about studying, since my midterm grades were barely able to maintain the C+ average I needed to stay in the engineering-physics curriculum. I remember having a particularly difficult time studying one night due to the heat when a distant roar of unquestionable human origin drew Bob and me from our study desks. Bob had a midterm exam and refused to leave the apartment to investigate the sound. I, however, couldn't run fast enough toward the ominous sound coming from Channing Circle in front of the Alpha Delta Pi sorority house, where I hashed.

As I ran up Channing Avenue past the Sigma Chi house, I approached the edge of a mass of students, all men, making unintelligible cries and hooting sounds. Making my way through the crowd, I discovered the head of the crowd surrounding the Alpha Delta Pi house trying to break through the locked front door. Inside, the girls had opened the front windows and were shouting back, taunting the crowd. With the crowd roaring and girls shouting, the air filled with an indistinguishable jumble of sounds. The crowd's objective quickly became obvious: break in and capture underwear from the girl's rooms while overcoming their weakly feigned resistance. It was a "panty raid!"

The mob packed against the front door. Feeling their heat, I joined in. Instead of pushing into the crowd, I made my way down the driveway to the Alpha Delta Pi back door we hashers used when entering and leaving the kitchen. Sure enough, the door was unlocked and no one was about. I guess I didn't think about what I was doing. I just ran inside through the gathering of coeds guarding the front door and, pushing my way to the door, opened it. In rushed the men, ignoring the girls and running up the stairs to the dormitory rooms, their quest apparent. I stepped back, beginning to think about what I'd done. Since I was so new to hashing at the Alpha Delta Pi house and still spent most of my time in the kitchen, none of the girls had called out my name, and I quickly slipped out the front door during the confusion.

I watched from across Channing Circle as some of the men came out of the house waving coeds' underwear to the roaring crowd, which was now forming an amoeba-like pseudopodium from its rear and moving north on Piedmont Avenue, seeking another victim. The human pseudopodium stopped in front of another sorority house, where it again halted by the locked front door, behind which the coeds jeered through the windows. My newly discovered talent of finding a way in led me to the rear of the house, looking for an unlocked door. Finding none, I spotted an open window on the second floor, leading into one of the rooms. And, *Aha*, there was an ideally placed, thin-trunked but climbable tree leading to the open window. There was no way I could resist. Up I went and through the window. Carefully crossing the room to the half-open door, I peered down into the living room.

It would be simple: just run down the stairs, cross the living room and open the door—just like before. All the sudden someone grasped me from behind, pinning my arms to my sides! A tall, surprisingly strong coed had me prisoner and proceeded to yell at the top of her lungs, "I got one! I got one!" For a couple seconds I was stunned. She must have been in the back of the room and watched me enter through the window. Instead of thwarting the entry, she let me in to affect the capture. Recovering, I broke loose and executed my mission as fast as possible. I left the house and decided that that was enough excitement for one night. On the way back to the apartment, I began to think about what I had done.

Was it right to become part of the mob the way I had? I could have just observed. What if someone had recognized me and reported me to the authorities as a vandal or worse? Had the crowd harmed anyone? Was there any significant damage? Was it worth it?

When I arrived back at the apartment, Bob was gone. Later, when he returned with a big grin on his face, I found out that he had been "bad" (his term). He had somehow "picked up" several lacy, white items during the evening and was in a quandary as to what to do with the loot. A couple of days later, a university review committee called him to answer questions concerning his whereabouts that evening. Coeds had identified several of the men in the mob in Channing Circle, and those who had participated by entering a sorority house faced discipline. Although Bob was better known around the sorority circuit than I, he somehow escaped punishment for his behavior.

The crowd probably petered out before long. I do not remember hearing details that indicated differently. Nor do I remember reading that the events of the night had led to any injury or significant damage. Of course, the girls complained, and I do remember hearing that there had been some minor damage reported. In their wisdom, University officials decided that it would be best if all the panties, and other items taken, were returned to their owners. A pile of panties and other unmentionables formed in the plaza outside the current Student Union a day or so after the raid, and female students were encouraged to recover their losses. This strategy did not work. The girls would just stand near the pile for a while and leave. The pile of panties disappeared a few days later.

Although panty raids by energetic male students had happened before, the evening of May 6, 1956, received the name "Great Panty Raid" in some press and achieved worldwide publicity as an example of student unrest and rebellion against the school administration. As I look back to that time, I am saddened to see how different the objectives and behavior of student groups were to become in the early 1960s. The relatively gentle panty raid of that night would not be possible once the more active and sometimes destructive student outcries against university authority became the campus norm. Little did I know that the entire nature of Cal was about to change.

The bohemian lifestyle, as the basis for the "Beat" culture, was not coined "beatnik" by Herb Caen until spring 1958. However, the "Beat" culture was what I found firmly established in Berkeley by the time I had arrived. Allen Ginsberg's poetry *Howl* had recently appeared in a small paperback, and Jack Kerouac was heavy in the SF street scene, with *On the Road* following the next year. Lawrence Ferlinghetti's *City Lights Bookstore* in San Francisco was a popular hangout for writers, artists, and musicians. I preferred the quiet ambiance of *Caffe Mediterraneum* (birthplace of the current caffè latte bar) on College Avenue and to later visit the *Blind Lemon* and *The Steppenwolf*, once located close together on San Pablo Avenue in Berkeley.

The change in crowd behavior that I am referring to is, I think, reflected in the morphing of beatniks into hippies. Whereas beats were mostly apolitical, relatively peaceful-natured, and more submissive to authority, hippies were actively engaged in civil issues and the later anti-war movement to the extent of being not just disruptive, but sometimes destructive with others' property. I witnessed firsthand the beginnings of this change with the formation of SLATE (not an acronym but a 'slate' of political candidates in 1958) and the start of the Free Speech Movement at Cal.

Returning to class after the pleasant but interruptive panty raid, I redoubled my study effort and backed away from the day-to-day social routines that dominated fraternity life. There were plenty of chances to fall prey to constant fun and games, and the added complication of hashing in a sorority house for meals did not help. The spring 1956 semester ended with no other disruptions of note that I can remember. My principal concern was that I had yet to establish contacts to help find a summer job and faced the prospect of soon returning home to San Diego. The discovery of a job advertisement in the *San Francisco Chronicle* was a godsend.

During the fall of 1957, I continued to work at NRDL part time. I learned that my group was preparing for atomic weapons tests in the Pacific during the spring and summer of 1958, making my work highly motivating and challenging. My work during the summer of 1957 and spring of 1958 at NRDL, which I describe later, provided a very different emotional surrounding, which competed with the college and fraternity life I just related.

It became a challenge to keep up my grades. Being able to study at the lab, after putting in my hours calculating radiation field levels, probably saved me from getting a disastrous grade point average. My combined office and laboratory at NRDL was a silent, windowless, constant-temperature environment, which helped me to concentrate. Although I had never been happier working, I was a bit sad facing the prospect that most of my group would be on an island in the Pacific during the summer, leaving me behind. Little did I know that, as the spring semester ended, the '58 summer I'd anticipated would not happen and what would take place would lead to my Armageddon experience.

I loved Berkeley and Cal and did not continue my earlier plan of moving on up the coast to the University of Washington. I continued the struggle for grades and finally received my BS in engineering physics in the spring of 1960, after failing a required physics class in optics, resulting in a delay graduating on time. I had already planned to spend the summer of '59 in Europe celebrating and was surprised when my grades arrived. I'd expected a "D" in optics, but not the "F" I'd received, and I had to return to take that one class and a couple of electives in the fall. Fortunately, my boss, Evan Evans, liked me, and failing optics and taking a summer in Europe did not interrupt the career I was beginning at NRDL.

CHAPTER 2

Naval Radiological Defense Laboratory

The horrific damage caused by nuclear weapons in Hiroshima and Nagasaki at the end of World War II took the U.S. population by surprise. The U.S. government's response was to begin testing these weapons in order to understand their use in warfare. Concurrently, the Department of Defense (DOD) questioned the potential risks nuclear weapons posed to our military troops and civilian population. National defense became the driving purpose behind the U.S. nuclear weapon test program until the Partial Test Ban Treaty of 1963 halted atmospheric testing.

After World War II, ever-increasing designs for nuclear weapon yields required the Navy to understand the wide range of issues the new type of weapons would have on fleet operations, personnel vulnerability, and their future in the country's strategic defense arsenal. The Naval Radiological Defense Laboratory was born during the earliest days of atmospheric testing, as part of the rapid development of these weapons for the Cold War.

U.S. Nuclear Weapon Atmospheric Testing

Within hours of the first successful nuclear detonation, codename Trinity, July 16, 1945, on the isolated northwest corner of the

Alamogordo desert bombing range in New Mexico, the cruiser *USS Indianapolis* left Hunters Point Naval Shipyard in San Francisco and sailed for the tiny Tinian Island in the western Pacific. Strapped to the deck in a fifteen-foot wooden crate was the gun assembly for *Little Boy* (named after its length was shortened from earlier designs, not for President Truman, as often rumored), the atomic bomb core used in the bombing of Hiroshima. Separately, two sailors aboard carried a Uranium (U^{235}) "bullet" in a lead bucket.

Little Boy had a high-tech brother: the implosion-type Plutonium (Pu^{239}) device that had been successfully proven in the Trinity test. It was code-named *Fat Man,* again rumored to be named for Winston Churchill, but more likely named after Sydney Greenstreet's character of "Kasper Gutman" in the movie *Maltese Falcon* because of its similar fat, round shape. *Fat Man's* nuclear assembly was a more difficult design than the U^{235} gun-barrel design strapped to the deck of the *USS Indianapolis*; which developed a critical mass simply by firing a piece of fissile material into a larger but slightly less critical piece. In *Fat Man,* the assembly achieved a sustainable fission reaction by compressing the Pu^{239} core with carefully coordinated explosions, increasing its density to the critical level. Today, the inefficient process used in *Little Boy,* which allowed the critical material to blow apart before reaching full explosive potential, is no longer used.

Pushed by the alarming progress made by the Soviet Union to create operational nuclear weapons, the Manhattan Project extended and expanded. Understanding of the underlying nuclear processes quickly evolved, and the engineering of smaller and more efficient designs accelerated. The Los Alamos Scientific Laboratory (LASL) and the Lawrence Livermore Laboratory competed to see which organization could make the weapons the military wanted. The result was a steady march toward the weapons of Armageddon that my NRDL summer job would eventually lead me to witness.

The fission process employed in nuclear power reactors to make electricity was not suitable for military purposes. *Little Boy* and *Fat Man* fission assembly designs were inherently limited to yields of about 1 megaton of explosive energy (1 MT). Even boosted Pu^{239} designs, where neutron production increases due to adding small amounts of other materials or reflecting some of the neutrons back into the core, faced similar yield limitations caused by explosive self-disassembly. Dr. Edward Teller argued for the "Super" process, where fission easily supplies the heat needed in the nuclear core to initiate much more energetic deuterium-tritium (isotopes of hydrogen) fusion (thermonuclear) reactions.[1] As nuclear weapon research progressed during the Cold War, the core and assembly designs produced smaller and lighter operational military weapons. By the time I witnessed Hardtack I *Oak* in 1958, a long series of nuclear weapons tests had been underway.

Even as early as the Trinity event, it was clear that the U.S. could not test such weapons within our continental boundaries. Hiroshima and Nagasaki had taught us that radioactive fallout from atmospheric tests posed a hazard far outside the intended target area. The search for a suitable area for atmospheric testing of nuclear weapon designs by the Atomic Energy Commission and the Navy understandably led them to the large, open, relatively unpopulated region of the western Pacific Ocean.

Fortunately, the U.S. had acquired administrative control of the Trust Territory of the Pacific Islands because of the Navy's thrust north from the Solomon Islands to Japan during World War II. The Marshall Islands District of the Trust Territory (Fig. 2) provided the relatively uninhabited open ocean area required for larger and larger detonations and their anticipated wind-disbursed radioactive fallout. Surely, the small native populations that inhabited some of the islands could be convinced to move from their homes for the good of the country that had saved them from Japanese domination. I learned later that the seemingly straightforward proposal that was the origin of the Pacific Proving Grounds was seriously flawed. I elaborate on those flaws and the issues that still exist in the Afterword.

U.S. nuclear weapons testing began with Operation Crossroads in the Bikini Atoll, located in the Pacific Proving Grounds, in July of 1946. Two nuclear weapon tests took place at Operation Crossroads: an

---

[1]   https://en.wikipedia.org/wiki/Operation_Crossroads.

airburst, like that from Hiroshima and Nagasaki, and an underwater burst that emulated its possible tactical use at sea against ships and submarines. (Many good resources on the web provide detailed information about Operation Crossroads. I have provided only summary background information here that relates to the establishment and mission of NRDL.)

Primarily a Navy exercise, the test targets for Operation Crossroads shots *Able* and *Baker* consisted of arrays of retired U.S. ships, as well as Japanese and German ships captured during the war.[2] (In the following text, specific nuclear detonations are italicized and referred to without their test series name, unless needed for clarification.) Anchored in a closely spaced flotilla in the shallow Bikini Atoll lagoon, the ships represented a lucrative target for an enemy. *Able* (Fig. 3), with a yield of 23,000 tons of TNT (23 KT), was detonated 520 feet above the target array. (From a distance in the field, nuclear weapon yield estimates are imprecise and usually depend on measurements from photos and various instruments recording fireball diameter, air pressure, and seismic wave magnitude.) The detonation resulted in several sunken ships and superstructure damage to a number of others. Radioactive fallout from bomb products in the gaseous plume was not serious, due to wind dispersion after the event. The limited overall damage to the flotilla that resulted was understandable, since ships are much stronger, and less vulnerable to fire, than the homes and structures found in Hiroshima and Nagasaki. The Navy was relieved.

Baker followed and had a similar yield but was an underwater burst, with the device suspended 90 feet below the surface, halfway to the lagoon bottom. This time the underwater shock wave caused structural damage to many of the ships, and compared to *Able,* a similar number of ships sank or were damaged. However, the above-surface plume generated from the detonation lifted some two million tons of seawater and sand into the air, creating a column 6,000 feet tall and 2,000 feet wide, with walls 300 feet thick (Fig. 4). When the column fell, it created

---

2   Rhodes, Richard, *Dark Sun: The Making of the Hydrogen Bomb*, (New York: Simon & Schuster), 1995.252.

a surge of water and mist 600 feet high, which quickly moved radially outward and engulfed most of the ships in the array. After everything settled, the Navy inherited a target fleet seriously contaminated by radioactive fission products, induced radionuclides, and Pu^{239}. The radioactive fallout impact on the flotilla was more destructive than had been predicted by Navy scientists.

Seamen immediately began decontamination practices known at the time: hosing down and scrubbing the ships with clean seawater and lye (Fig. 5). This resulted in the spread of contaminated seawater, producing such a severe exposure to so many of the workers that Operation Crossroads was terminated early two weeks later and the deep-water shot (*Charlie*) planned for spring 1947 was canceled. Scientists estimated that in a fully manned fleet, with no effective decontamination procedures available, most of the 35,000 sailors would eventually die from the exposure to the radioactive material spread over the ships by the base surge. The Navy faced the prospect that in nuclear warfare at sea, as they understood it, a single, rather low-yield nuclear bomb might be able to destroy the effectiveness of an entire fleet!

At the time, this was an exaggerated account of the potential damage to a fleet. In normal operations at sea, ships are not as closely spaced as they were during Operation Crossroads, and the base surge would not have engulfed as large a fraction of the fleet. Nor would ships be moored. Some ships would be able to maneuver quickly away from the radioactive cloud produced and reduce their radiation exposure. However, the prospect of much larger thermonuclear weapons under development underscored the lack of understanding about the damage to ships from such weapons and weighed heavily on the future of naval operations against a sophisticated enemy like the Soviet Union.

Partial Test Ban Treaty

As thermonuclear weapon yields reached multi-megaton levels, the destructive power and the extent of radioactive fallout were just some of the expanded concerns now faced by war planners and politicians.

Smaller, more efficient designs were developed that could be packaged into multiple warhead delivery vehicles. Efficiency, size, and weight dominated the development and testing effort. (Table 1 provides a short summary of the U.S. open-air atmospheric tests that took place at the Pacific Proving Grounds before international pressure forced their termination.) The Soviet Union competed with the U.S. with similar atmospheric and underwater nuclear weapons tests throughout this period. Their weapon tests included even greater yields, possibly for use against cities and population centers (see Tsar Bomba test in Chapter 9).

As early as the 1950s, the Soviet Union proposed limiting the development and testing of nuclear weapons. A major problem with the negotiations arose when deciding how testing high-yield weapons would be regulated. This problem remained an obstacle for negotiations until 1959, when testing and requirements became separate issues. By 1961, the discussion centered on clandestine underground testing, which was (and still is) difficult to monitor without local inspection of the test site. The U.S., Great Britain, and the Soviet Union signed a Partial Test Ban Treaty in July 1953. Finally, in 1963, Premier Khrushchev agreed to the U.S. position to limit all testing except that which could be contained underground. This banned all nuclear testing in the atmosphere, underwater, and in outer space.

Atmospheric and outer space nuclear tests are relatively easy to detect, and the 1963 treaty has been highly successful among the signatories, although there has always been some discussion of clandestine underwater tests in the deep ocean being possible. Unfortunately, China, France, and North Korea did not sign the treaty and carried out atmospheric nuclear tests after 1963. Additionally, there have been two cases of radioactivity leaks from underground tests: one from the Soviet Union in 1965 and one from the U.S. in Nevada in 1970. Although denied, Israel may have conducted an atmospheric weapon test in 1979 in the southern Indian Ocean.[3]

---

[3]   http://nuclearweaponarchive.org/Usa/Tests/Crossrd.html.

Early Days of the Naval Radiological Defense Laboratory

Local attempts to decontaminate the ship targets at Operation Crossroads failed miserably, and many of the ships ended up scuttled in deep water far outside Bikini Atoll or towed to Navy facilities at Pearl Harbor and Puget Sound. Fourteen heavily contaminated ships and submarines ended up at the Hunters Point Naval Shipyard in San Francisco. A rag-tag group of junior naval officers, fresh from being radiation monitors at Operation Crossroads, followed the ships to Hunters Point. They set up laboratories in two small, poorly instrumented rooms at the Hunters Point Naval Shipyard, where they formally assembled for radiological studies.[4]

The Naval Radiological Defense Laboratory was born on November 18, 1946; their mission from the Navy was to study physical, chemical, and biological effects of radiation generated from nuclear weapons. Although initially focused on the decontamination of the Operation Crossroads vessels, the Navy quickly recognized the need to include physicists, chemists, and biologists in the staff to meet the challenges of the broader mission.

The number of people and buildings required to house and support the scientists, medical doctors, and engineers and their equipment rapidly grew. Extensive efforts at the shipyard, even under the scientists' oversight, to rid the ships of radioactive material had proved more difficult than originally thought. Chemical scrubbing failed to efficiently remove radioactive particles, which transferred to the algae and other plant life that clung to the outer hull and deck surfaces. A number of decontamination studies on specimens removed from contaminated ships found that sandblasting followed by chemical washing was more effective. However, the process spread fine radioactive particulate far

---

4   Davis, Lisa, "FALLOUT," *SF Weekly*, May 28, 2001 (sfweekly.com). A two-part series of investigative research done by Ms. Davis provides a detailed description of the problems associated with conducting research on decontamination of the Operation Crossroads ships. Her articles focus on the contamination of the Hunters Point Shipyard and surrounding impact on the bay and reclamation of the land for civilian use after the shipyard closed.

beyond the shipyard decontamination site. In addition, contaminated particles drawn into a ship's interior spread throughout most of the compartments. Eventually, ships too extensively contaminated to salvage ended up scuttled off the Farallon Islands, 27 miles outside the Golden Gate Bridge.

Within a year or two, over 20 buildings scattered around the shipyard housed decontamination activities. By 1950, it became clear that a dedicated facility was required to house and unify the massive effort needed to understand nuclear warfare at sea. In addition, understanding the radiation hazard to the civilian population as well as to military personnel in land-based facilities was critical.

Naval Radiological Defense Laboratory, Building 815

I worked in NRDL, Building 815 (Fig. 1), the newly constructed main research laboratory built by the Navy at Hunters Point in response to the growing need to understand the radiological effects of nuclear weapons. The Hunters Point Naval Shipyard juts into the San Francisco Bay about ten miles south of downtown San Francisco and was a major ship repair facility for the Navy during World War II. Building 815 stood out in contrast to the older shipyard buildings. It was a light grey concrete structure, a little over 400 feet long and 100 feet wide, not in itself unusual for a research building; however, it was also six stories high without a single window. The building interior was a self-contained, controlled environment designed for security from outside snooping that additionally provided an extremely efficient facility for research and for handling radioactive material. Building 815, occupied for only two years, was new when I arrived.

Answering the call from scientists trying to decontaminate Operation Crossroads target ships, the Navy Bureau of Ships solicited 14 million dollars from Congress to build a new laboratory to integrate many of the temporary laboratories that had sprung up across the shipyard. An architectural firm was hired, and a design of the new laboratory building was briefed to a group of NRDL officers and scientists. It was a three-story building with wings projecting from the back, giving nearly every worker a combined office/laboratory with a window.[5] A lively discussion with NRDL scientists followed, and their design was totally rejected.

The scientists suggested the architects return to the drawing board and come back with a six-story concrete, windowless blockhouse that would provide the secrecy and safety needed to conduct experiments with radioactive material. I do not fault the architects completely. In 1950, few architects understood the combined radiological hazard and security requirements of such a military laboratory. Civilian research laboratories could be more academically oriented and open to the public.

A new design was developed. However, it would exceed the current budget and resulted in a decision to decrease the building's overall length, but to retain the recommended six floors. Fortunately, the final bid was below budget. Unable, at this point, to modify the current plans, a separate building was added alongside the bid version, returning NRDL to the original design the scientists required for their clandestine research. This resulted in some internal asymmetry for elevator locations but was satisfactory in every other way to the scientists. (In my ten years spent running around the six floors, I never noticed that NRDL consisted of two separate buildings.)

Construction on NRDL Building 815 began in 1952 and was dedicated in the fall of 1955. The building cost eight million dollars and, at the time, was one of the world's most modern and best-equipped nuclear research laboratories. The remainder of the funds provided by Congress went to providing the lab with the best instrumentation available anywhere in the world. Working at NRDL with access to seemingly unlimited equipment and a dedicated mission in the defense of one's country was a dream come true.

NRDL instrumentation included high-intensity gamma radiation sources and X-ray machines, scintillation spectrometers, multi-channel

---

[5]   Strope, W.E, (circa 1994), "Chapter 8, The Nerd in NRDL" p.107. Unpublished autobiography, available in various chapters at http://www.thriftywebsites.us/stropesus/mom&dad/autobiography.htm.

differential analyzers, high-speed calorimeters and bolometers, ultracentrifuges, radiation counters, spectrographs, spectrophotometers, electron microscopes, climatic simulators, master/slave manipulators for handling radioactive material, and engineering equipment. Utility outlets located along the wall workbenches in most of the individual laboratories included AC and DC power, compressed air, distilled water, vacuum, steam, and natural gas.[6] Special hooded laboratory spaces with venting to control gaseous emissions were located in the back corners of each of the laboratory rooms.

NRDL Operational Structure

Building 815 had a unique working environment, operational structure, and internal organization. It housed a major research laboratory that integrated widely different technical disciplines focused on a singular mission. Although the existence and mission of NRDL was not classified information, I recall that the public throughout the Bay Area was surprisingly unaware of the work carried out in Building 815.

Looking back now, I still find the operational structure of NRDL unique. Employing about 500 people within the building, nearly half research scientists and half support staff, NRDL was managed by a combined military commanding officer (Captain, USN), and technical director (PhD). NRDL's major divisions of technical expertise were:[7]

> Nucleonics– Research into ionizing radiation sources and shielding of nuclear and thermal radiation for the purpose of developing and calibrating radiation-monitoring instrumentation.

---

[6]   Hinners, Captain Robert A., USN (retired), August 1957, "History of the U.S. Naval Radiological Defense Laboratory- An Insurance Policy for the Atomic Future," 1946-58, *J. Am. Soc. For Naval Eng.*, 69, Issue 3, 417–438. (ACHRE No. DOD-071494-A-1). Capt. Hinners was the first Commanding Officer of Building 815. NRDL published this article during the summer of my first employment at the lab.

[7]   Ibid.

> Chemical Technology– Research on creating and transporting nuclear weapon radiation, developing decontamination processes, and environmental impact assessments.
>
> Biomedical Division – Field and laboratory research on the effects of ionizing and thermal radiation on small and large animals. Developing radiological countermeasures, safety procedures, and equipment.
>
> Military Evaluations Group – Assess military effectiveness of radiological defense and civilian defense against nuclear weapons.

The purpose and mission of the divisions embedded an overriding emphasis on defense as opposed to offensive use of nuclear weapons. A close cooperation with all U.S. military services, government agencies and laboratories, universities, and foreign allies made NRDL a major international center for radiological defense research.

Integrating the six floors of the building significantly reduced the physical security required A guard at the shipyard south gate posed the first barrier by requiring ID and a car pass. Another guard faced us down when entering the main entrance on the first floor, requiring further ID and providing a numbered film badge to measure any radiation exposure we might receive while at work. Once beyond the entry guard post, we were able to move to the central stack of escalators that could take us to our floor.

NRDL film badges contained of a piece of photographic film with special emulsions designed to increase its sensitivity, covered by various metal and plastic filters to pass a measured amount of radiation from gamma rays, electrons, and neutrons. Early film badges, as used in Operation Crossroads, were only able to detect gamma rays and missed much of the potentially dangerous exposure the clean-up crews faced. Alpha particles consist of two protons and two neutrons and are too large and heavy to penetrate even the thinnest covering, rendering the Crossroads film badges useless for measuring their presence. However, at the molecular level, inside living tissue, alpha particle ionization can be disastrous to cell survival. Once calibrated, the later film badges provided a more reliable (but after-exposure) estimate of the amount of radiation we received.

Since NRDL workspaces were carefully monitored for uncontrolled radioactive material, film badges were "read" periodically to record workers' gamma radiation exposure history while inside Building 815. Nowadays, thermoluminescent dosimeters are available, which indicate the exposure level by measuring the temperature rise when a crystal is heated by the energy it absorbs as the ionizing particle passes through.

My permanent office was on the sixth floor, along with the others in the Chemical Technology Division. Dr. Evan C. Evan's group was located down the southeast hall, where I shared one of the larger rooms that first summer in 1957. The sixth floor was crowded with radiochemists, and their instruments, studying the radiation spectrum and chemistry associated with bomb fission products and induced radionuclides as part of a decontamination process. Their research complemented my group's mission, which was preparing for physical measurement of the radiation fields anticipated during the Pacific weapons tests during the next summer (1958). The west end of the sixth floor also contained a 300-seat auditorium used for all-hands announcements and technical seminars. I practiced my technical talks alone on the stage in the darkened auditorium many times and once gave a seminar on the statistical aspects of the direction of time. Our technical director allowed seminar topics far from our current research.

The fifth floor housed biological and medical laboratories for conducting research using a variety of small (and some larger) animals. Biomedical Division's objective was to study tissue damage and loss of performance as animals received different levels and types of nuclear radiation. The laboratories were well-equipped and staffed by highly qualified scientists and medical doctors, dedicated to determining how to best protect and treat people who had been exposed. Today, animal rights activists would undoubtedly not approve of many of the activities that took place on the fifth floor, as well as the tests involving animal subjects in the nuclear weapons field tests in the Pacific and Nevada. However, the data from research using animals at NRDL, and other similar laboratories, have produced better protection for our military personnel and contributed to radiation exposure standards now found throughout civilian society.

On the fourth floor, physicists and engineers built and tested new nuclear and thermal radiation detection instruments to monitor radioactive contamination occurring during both civilian nuclear accidents and on the battlefield. In one of the larger laboratories, a large carbon arc simulated the heat from a nuclear weapon to measure the effects of thermal radiation on various materials. I remember placing my hand in the thermal beam once to feel a low exposure level and then exposing a thick piece of aluminum to see the melted hole a more intense beam could produce. Another part of the fourth floor contained a Van de Graaff accelerator that provided a beam of electrons to study the effects of radiation on the solid-state electronics used by the military.

I saved some samples from the fourth floor showing the damage radiation weapons could cause to various materials. Several years later, I carried them with me when briefing Navy program officers on the effects of directed energy laser and particle beam weapons. Once, I showed a ¼-inch thick piece of aluminum with the half-inch melt hole to a visiting Marine Corps general, who quickly understood what such a beam of thermal energy might do to his helicopters. I also saved a block of clear plastic showing a frozen, forked lightning-like path of melted material, created by the beam from our Van de Graaff accelerator. Later in my career, while working for the Lawrence Livermore National Laboratory (LLNL), I used the visible path of the electron beam in the plastic block to demonstrate how the inside of a high-explosive warhead of an incoming missile might be prematurely detonated when hit by an electron beam weapon.

Support Facilities and Activities

The cafeteria was located on the roof of Building 815 for a good reason. Since the building was windowless, the scientists and architects designing the building decided we needed a place to periodically escape from our work and join the rest of humanity. It turned out to be a good idea, since there would later be rumors of an unusually high suicide rate among Building 815 employees. We speculated that there must be something about the rooms causing people to freak out after long hours in partial confinement. Engineers carefully measured room dimensions to determine whether there was a slight skew in their geometry that somehow might affect the brain and induce suicidal thoughts. (I believe that a team of psychologists considered the problem, but there was no evidence supporting the rumors.) The cafeteria provided a welcome respite from work confinement, and we enjoyed brief breaks and a 30-minute lunchtime looking out over the San Francisco Bay's South Basin, what was to become Candlestick Park, and further to Brisbane to the southwest.

The third floor housed the library and a Burroughs 650 mainframe computer. This was in a time before personal computers, and the facility was used to compile programs and make punch cards—then wait overnight for the results, which often said, "Recompile." We never got the IBM 704 we wanted. At my desk, I used a Marchant 10-bank and an 18-inch slide rule.

The commanding officer and technical director offices and some management functions were also located on the third floor. Because of their direct staff support to the commanding officer and technical director, the Military Evaluation Division, which conducted investigations on the longer-term strategic aspects of nuclear warfare, were adjacent.

The second floor was another favorite area for hanging out. For years after I returned from Operation Hardtack, I spent considerable time in the student machine shop, where I could use the smaller tools to build the research equipment I needed. Master machinists from the main machine shop on the first floor, where they fabricated larger and more complex equipment, oversaw our attempts to build the equipment. Working in the shop was a learning experience, as master machinists taught me how to use a drill press, lathe, milling machine, and other power tools. I believed that some of the complex first-floor machine tools were German manufactured and acquired after the war, and I wondered if some of the machinists might be German immigrants as well.

Roy Bryant's glass-blowing shop on the second floor was always an interesting place to visit. He supplied the chemists with intricate, unusual glass structures and maintained a veritable museum of fascinating items that were obviously fabricated by a fine craftsman. But my favorite area, by far, was Shop Stores, a.k.a., the supermarket, where aisle-upon-aisle was filled with an unbelievable assortment of electronics, hardware, hand tools, and other sundry items constantly needed during research. I could check out all of these "goodies" for my work with a signature and project charge number. Although I did not use these facilities that first summer in 1957, they all became indispensable later in my time at NRDL.

Finally, there was one occupant of the second floor that made NRDL different from any other laboratory I experienced in my long research career: Katie Young in Contract Services. Katie stands out in my mind. To her, quickly finding and purchasing items needed for our research was a personal goal. If you knew what you needed for your project and could not find it in the supermarket, you went to see Katie. If you needed the item in a hurry, she would call the vendor while you waited, place the order, and give you a delivery date. I have never since experienced that level of support during my research.

CHAPTER 3

Summer of 1957

Everything was new to me that summer of 1957: a new place to work, new friends and colleagues, and a work environment beyond anything I had ever dreamed of. Moreover, as it turned out, I would never again, in all my years conducting and directing high-tech research and development projects for the Navy enjoy such a unique laboratory.

As I indicated earlier, I do not remember the details of my job interview with Tak Shirasawa, Evan's engineering assistant, or any particulars about why I got the job. I was probably the first, or only one, to apply. When I reported for work in June, Tak took me in tow. He showed me our laboratory spaces, introduced me to too many future colleagues to remember, and found a desk for me to occupy for the summer. The Chemical Technology Division (Code 930) dominated most of the sixth floor; Tak was in the Radiological Effects Branch (Code 934), which provided field support for the division. He was, and still is, an easygoing type-B personality who never appears to be upset or agitated by others, events, or situations. I remember him describing some of the idiosyncrasies of my new boss, Evan Cyfeiliog Evans III, who was away for the moment. Apparently, he was a fireball of energy—just the opposite of Tak.

Freed from classes and the routine of hashing, I concentrated on studying the technology of nuclear weapons effects, i.e., what happens to the environment and to radioactive material after detonation. Since NRDL was a Navy laboratory, the emphasis was on warfare at sea, and specifically low-yield underwater nuclear weapons to fire from U.S. ships and submarines against Soviet vessels.

***

My task that first summer was to become familiar with underwater nuclear weapons effects and learn how to calculate the gamma radiation fields associated with the detonation debris. Later that summer, I helped determine where to place instruments to measure the distribution of radioactive material as it spread over the ocean surface. The Radiological Effects Branch was responsible for designing field experiments to measure the radiation fields from two underwater nuclear bursts planned for an exercise in the summer of 1958 called Operation Hardtack I. I was stoked! How could anyone ask for a better summer job?

When Evan returned, a hurricane of task assignments engulfed me. Suddenly I was so busy I couldn't see straight and was deep in over my head trying to make calculations of gamma radiation exposure, as a function of time, near massive radioactive geometrical shapes that were moving. At the time, I did not understand how those shapes related to underwater nuclear detonations. Evan guided me in the work, and with access to some earlier reports, I managed to struggle through the summer. Tak was right; Evan was a sort of brilliant eccentric who somehow always commanded your respect. He was about 5'10", 170 pounds with black, unkempt hair and intense dark eyes—not a penetrating kind of burning but sparkling and full of life. He appeared to be about ten years older than I was.

Several of my new colleagues lived in Berkeley. Evan was in a large, brown-shingle house in a beautiful, heavily foliated area south of Ashby Avenue above College Avenue. Tak lived high above Berkeley on Grizzly Peak Boulevard, and Ed Schuert and Charlie Adams were along the route up to Tak's house. Evan and his wife, Joanie, adopted me as a lost, away-from-home student and invited me to dinners and holiday parties. Evan accepted me as a young colleague over the next few years, becoming a mentor, both as I entered the world of nuclear weapons research and in an unusual social/intellectual environment that lay beyond science, which I will describe in a later chapter.

UC Berkeley and its associated Lawrence Livermore Laboratory (now Lawrence Livermore National Laboratory), located east of the Oakland hills toward the town of Tracy, and the Los Alamos Scientific Laboratory designed, built, and tested the bombs, while we, who worked for the Navy, conducted field tests to measure what happened after they were detonated at sea. We were at war with the Soviet Union—a cold, slow-moving, physical, but real war. This was heady stuff for a kid in school who spent most of his time socializing with fraternity brothers and coeds. I lived a secret life far away from my classes and fraternity brothers, which I could not let on about other than "it's classified."

Before I arrived, NRDL personnel had participated in a number of nuclear weapons tests at the Pacific Proving Grounds that followed Operation Crossroads. The most recent was Operation Redwing in 1956 (Table 1). One hundred seven NRDL civilians had participated in nearly a dozen different technical projects over years of testing. By far the largest NRDL project involved fallout characterization, on which I was working. Bob Hammond, Tom Dahlstrom, Norm Alvarez, and other of my fourth-floor colleagues worked on projects measuring thermal radiation.

Tak and others told me that Operation Redwing was a particularly difficult series of tests because it was the first time an aircraft dropped a thermonuclear bomb. Operation Redwing *Cherokee* missed its aim point by four miles, placing test personnel in danger of radiation exposure. Other Operation Redwing tests experimented with "dirty" (highly radioactive fallout) fission-fusion device designs creating very high-yield, somewhat-unpredictable detonations that complicated predictions of where the fallout would end up. It seemed to me at the time that there was some significant danger of exposure to serious levels of radiation while participating in nuclear tests!

During Hardtack I, our group would be responsible for measuring radiation fallout from Shot *Wahoo* and Shot *Umbrella*, the only underwater nuclear detonations included in the test series. *Wahoo* and

Umbrella were to be the most extensively instrumented underwater
nuclear detonations in the world to date, and they actually still retain
that distinction. We formulated the first experiments to measure the
radioactive products immediately surrounding the detonations and
provide the data required to estimate the risk to a nearby Navy fleet.

The plans for Hardtack I consisted of 33 shots distributed between
Enewetak and Bikini Atolls from April 28 to August 18, 1958.
("Enewetak," adopted in 1974 in place of "Eniwetok," better represents
the native pronunciation.) Two high-altitude shots would also take
place above Johnson Island, about 900 miles west of Hawaii. Hardtack
I would release a total of 35.6 megatons (MT) of nuclear warheads
and experimental devices during the test series (Table 2). Shots *Wahoo*
and *Umbrella* were fission weapons ready for deployment to the Navy.[8]
A series of smaller nuclear detonations took place during Operation
Hardtack II, which followed the Pacific series, at the Nevada Test Site.
I found myself involved in something BIG—and important.

Some of the instrumentation we were building would collect samples
of the fallout as a function of time (rate) and total amount at various
distances from the detonation on the water surface. Other instruments
would measure the gamma radiation intensity levels (R/hr, see glossary)
and total dose (R) accumulated. I was tasked with exercising my new
university-acquired math skills to calculate the gamma radiation fields
that begin seconds after the burst. I finally found out why I had been
learning to do calculations using moving ideal geometrical shapes; they
represented the radioactive plume and base surge that formed above the
detonation.

Although I was primarily learning to calculate gamma radiation
fields, my first summer at NRDL provided a general education regarding
underwater nuclear explosions. For example, I learned how the bubble
produced by a 10-kiloton (KT) explosion set off beneath a destroyer
could completely lift it out of the water, possibly breaking it in two.

---

8   http://nuclearweaponarchive.org/Usa/Tests/Hardtack1.html, and "Technical
     summary of Military Effects Programs 1-9," Operation Hardtack Preliminary
     Report, (1959), Interim Technical Report sanitized version (1999), pdf.

I learned some of the physics of how the plume and column fall back to the surface, forming a surge of mist that carries radioactive fission products miles downwind from the blast. It was scary but exciting to think of. I contributed little that was original or particularly useful to the project that first summer: I was receiving a broader education about nuclear war.

I began to absorb some of the physics involved, and how various underwater phenomena varied with weapon yield, detonation depth, and water depth related to what happened above the surface. I recalled the submarine attack scenes in movies of World War II submarine warfare I had seen. I had always wondered what happened within the visible black residue that remained in the water after a depth charge explosion. I later saw the movie *Run Silent, Run Deep* and began to understand how underwater explosion bubbles formed and moved in the water column. However, it was not until after Hardtack I, when I studied the theory associated with underwater explosions, that I understood how the depth charge bubbles I saw formed and that they could sometimes migrate upward, downward, and even sideways in the water after an explosion.

I also read about World War II and the development of the atomic bomb and the why and how of the horrible bombings of Hiroshima and Nagasaki. My curiosity was peaked when my mother told me that she had worked on *Enola Gay* (the plane that delivered the Hiroshima atomic bomb) once she knew of my work at NRDL. Mom had worked at Convair Corporation in San Diego, which helped provide my parents with spare money for a college car and living expenses for their son. Before we moved to San Diego, Mom had been an inspector at the Glenn Martin Company Bellevue plant south of Omaha during World War II. She was small framed and able to crawl into confined spaces in the bombers Martin built, including the B-29 Superfortress, *Enola Gay*. Colonel Paul Tibbets Jr., the pilot for the Tokyo mission, had been commander of the 509th Composite Group. He'd selected the airframe on May 9, 1945, while it was still on the assembly line, and named it *Enola Gay* after his mother.

The airframe was one of 15 B-29s with the "Silverplate" modifications necessary to deliver an atomic weapon.[9] The Hiroshima bomb, "Little Boy," weighed about 10,000 pounds. Due to its size and weight, the aircraft bomb bay needed extensive alterations, sacrificing heavy protective armor and the gun turrets. Although Mom and the other workers did not know its intended mission, they knew there was something special about that particular airframe because of the excessive attention it received during construction and inspection.

As the summer of 1957 progressed, I fell into a pleasant, stimulating daily life at NRDL. Every day was exciting; I was never late to work and often stayed late. Even lunch was informative and fun. It was a time to get to know colleagues better and learn about their personal lives. Two older colleagues were particularly interesting. Not being naturally gregarious, I probably needed an introduction to Dr. Newell and Dr. Schwob one day when joining a larger group at one of the dining tables.

Dr. Robert Newell was much older than the rest of us, and his white hair and conspicuous white lab coat, which most of us removed at lunch, were consistent with my view of a scientist, especially one recognized for his standing as a radiologist in the international nuclear community. To me, he appeared ancient. Dr. Newell worked as a consultant to NRDL, and although he presented the aura of an elder statesman, he was always outgoing and talkative. He especially impressed me one day when he graciously reacted to a trick we played on him while eating and conversing around our table.

Dr. Newell (I never mustered up the courage to call him by his first name, as some of the others did) wore hearing aids in both ears and graciously accepted the nickname "Stereo." In those days, hearing aids were large, obvious earbuds. The pocketed controls needed constant tweaking to adjust sensitivity and background noise filtering levels. One day, we all decided before his arrival to lower our voices slowly while carrying on a normal conversation with each other. As the conversation volume dropped, Stereo kept turning up the volume of his hearing aids so he could follow the discussion. Then on cue, the conversation

<hr>

9   https://en.wikipedia.org/wiki/Silverplate.

suddenly returned to a normal volume. Stereo jumped up and cursed his hearing aid controls, then turned to us and smiled. We all laughed. Dr. Newell left NRDL shortly after I arrived, and I never had the chance to know him better than the occasional discussions in the cafeteria. During that short time, I learned to appreciate his knowledge and experience.

I noticed that my earlier notion that scientists were always serious and staid was not true. They all did not look like Einstein! My new colleagues sometimes behaved like my fraternity brothers. They were real people, like my dad and his friends, and they liked to play tricks on one another.

Dr. Claude Schwob, a consummate radiochemist, was completely different from my other colleagues but highly respected in his field of expertise. Claude had worked on the Manhattan Project and was now at NRDL helping develop the decontamination technology we were trying to understand. He too was much older than I was and was unabashedly gay.

Claude lived in San Francisco while following a completely open gay lifestyle and talked explicitly about his weekend nude parties and boyfriends, just as the rest of us talked about some of our after work family activities. I never perceived any ill feelings toward Claude within the lab because of his sexual orientation and later found out that he had been similarly treated and respected during his days with the Manhattan Project. Gays were trying to make important contributions to national security like the rest of us at NRDL. I still clearly remember Claude and his explicitly narrated lifestyle, and I value his contribution to my understanding and total acceptance of homosexuality as an alternative lifestyle. Claude is eulogized in an untitled San Francisco art film.[10]

I worked through the summer of 1957 at NRDL and lived alone in South San Francisco in a small, one-room flat. My work on gamma radiation fields was progressing, as was my more general education in

[10] Elliot Anderson, a media artist living in San Francisco at the time, became intrigued by Claude's ability to fit into the scientific community while leading such an outwardly gay, erotic lifestyle and years later eulogized him in an art film. http://www.queerculturealcenter.org/Pages/Chrono/Anderson.html.

nuclear weapons effects. For example, "How do you estimate the yield of a nuclear weapon while watching one go off some distance away and evaluate the potential danger from the associated thermal pulse?" (It is not good to be too near. I am a relatively fast learner and got that point right away, after seeing photos of burn victims in Hiroshima.) Other basic back-of-the-envelope rules on shockwave magnitude, water wave height, etc. were also absorbed during my studies. (Chapter 8 provides another level of detail.)

During that summer, I read as many NRDL lab reports as I could find. The biological effects of radiation and the exposure levels humans can tolerate without serious injury were particularly interesting. For example, our early instruments, like the NRDL film pack dosimeter, gave a simple total exposure from gamma radiation (similar to but more energetic than X-rays) and were valuable for after-the-event estimates of how an exposed person is treated. On the other hand, a handheld Geiger counter measured the rate of exposure from ionizing radiation that could be caused by a beta particle (an electron), an alpha particle (two neutrons and two protons), and free neutron fluxes. Geiger counters were invaluable for identifying the instantaneous level of exposure from ionizing radiation like gamma rays so you could determine when to run for cover.

The radiation we feared most was in situations of total body exposure to gamma rays. (If the following couple of paragraphs appear tedious, stick with it. It is important later when I discuss the effects nuclear weapons would have if detonated on the U.S. and in particular, over San Francisco.) Dose was measured using units called Roentgens (R), which specifies the amount of ionizing radiation that is needed to generate a given electric charge in air at standard temperature and pressure. Shortly after Operation Hardtack, the units rad and rem were introduced to distinguish the ionization effects on materials other than air. The unit rem (Roentgen equivalent man) is still found in medical literature since it denotes the amount of ionizing radiation applicable to human tissue density and absorption characteristics. Nowadays, the unit sievert (1 Sv = 100 rem) is the International System of Units (SI) definition of dose equivalent radiation commonly used to describe the exposure level in humans. The unit sievert is now common when citing exposure level for workers in nuclear power reactor accidents.

According to the Environmental Protection Agency, the average exposure from normal background radiation now in the U.S. is 0.3 rem in a year and 0.006 rem during an average high-altitude flight across the continent. The annual dose limit for workers at nuclear plants in the U.S. is 5 rem/year. If one accumulates 10 rem (30 years of background), lab tests would be able to detect some change in one's tissue from the ionizing radiation received. Noticeable physical effects are unlikely.

On the other end of the scale, nausea can begin when you are exposed to about 50 rem, and tissue hemorrhaging can be clinically noticed at 100 rem. On average, 50% of the people exposed to 500 rem of ionizing radiation, who do not receive medical treatment, die within 30 days. And things get worse at higher exposure levels. However, both the exposure situation and treatment immediately after exposure can significantly mitigate the above effects.

***

Finally, summer ended and I returned to Berkeley for my junior year. Since returning to my former digs when classes began was not possible, my former roommate Bob Shugert and I searched the want ads for a new place to stay. Good apartments were difficult to find, but luckily, we found a one-bedroom flat in an old redwood house built shortly after the 1906 San Francisco earthquake. Mike Mote, another fraternity brother, joined us and we moved into a spacious apartment that was perched off the northwest side of Panoramic Hill, overlooking Strawberry Canyon and the Cal Stadium. The address, 38 Mosswood, was at the bottom of long, steep stairs leading up to the house. We had the largest of three apartments in the house, with access from Arden Circle from above that provided some daily convenience but no parking space. Everyone living on Panoramic Hill faced a grueling climb on foot from campus.

The views were spectacular and fundamentally ruined me forever in terms of where I want to live. Is there a view? Is it facing west for the sunset? Our new pad consisted of a small bedroom with single beds, a kitchen, and a large living room with a fireplace and deck from which we could look down into the stadium. The walls of the living room were redwood, and there was a large, solid wood table in a niche surrounded on three sides with windows facing the Bay. On many nights I would place a soft chair on the table and read, to watch the light reflected off the bay as the sun set and then disappear as night slowly approached. After a while, I could almost tell the time of night by the loss of color from the neon lights in the pulsating civilization below.

Miss Andrews, our landlady, lived on the north side of campus. She had lived in the house we rented with her family in the early 1900s. I never knew how old she was, but to the three of us, she was ancient. She told us stories about how her family accumulated their soiled linens and sent them to China for laundering after the 1906 San Francisco earthquake. She would visit on the first of the month to collect $35 rent from each of us. Upon arriving, she would call out "Yoohoo, yoohoo, boys, boys..." several times in her high voice. We would run and hide in a small space behind the wall of a closet we had found to avoid her talking a leg off.

Once, when two of us were home, I was not able to get into the hideout in time when she called out. Panic stricken, I got into bed, pulled the covers over my clothes, and pretended to be asleep. After searching through the house, she finally came into the bedroom, discovered me, and put her face close enough to mine that her facial hair tickled my cheek. She said, "I know you are awake. You can't fool me." Then she turned around and left! She really was a good sport, and if we did not have the rent, we could always have an extra day or two to come up with it.

I did not work the fall semester at NRDL, but I kept in touch with Tak and followed project efforts for Operation Hardtack I. Christmas vacation came, and I was able to work full time over the holidays. I caught up on the technical details of the instrumentation and the theoretical calculations needed to support the fieldwork the team was planning for the summer tests. After holiday break, I started working at the lab half time and was able to get more involved in estimating the gamma radiation fields expected from the water column and base surge.

I really wanted to go on the operation but expected to keep colleagues who were not going company in San Francisco throughout the 1958 summer. The team departed NRDL in April and I felt left out after doing so much work predicting the data they would measure.

I received little information regarding the team's efforts and how things were going. Fortunately, I had classes to worry about and thought little about what I was missing. Then one day I found out that I could go! It was getting late in the Hardtack I test series on Enewetak Atoll and there were instrument problems during Shot *Wahoo*, the first detonation for our project. Evan sent a message that he needed me to help prepare for *Umbrella*, the next underwater burst. Things happened fast. My departure date was before spring final exams, and I needed permission from each professor to take a make-up exam upon my return. I went to them one-by-one and explained the work I did at NRDL and about the opportunity offered me. To the man, they promised they would be available upon my return later in the summer to give me individual exams, since the experience I would gain would be so worthwhile. I would receive an incomplete for each class at the end of the semester and receive the grade later after the final exam in time for beginning the fall semester. The prospect of six final exams during the summer and missing the latest lectures and study discipline imposed by classmates was daunting, but what an opportunity for a lowly Cal junior.

I rushed through a series of immunization shots, and the Air Force at Sandia Base cut ten copies of my orders to Enewetak Island. I received the status of a Navy Commander to facilitate travel within the military system. *Umbrella* would take place in June, 150 feet below the surface, with a modest yield. I felt that *Umbrella* belonged to me. With help from more experienced scientists who had participated in earlier tests and the earlier high-explosive test data I had seen, I knew how it would look from every vantage point: underwater, on the surface, and from 10,000 feet in the air. I had made estimates of the radiation emitted from radioactive material raised in the plume as it fell back and spread away from surface zero in the base surge and finally from the radioactive pool that remained.

I left Berkeley for Enewetak Atoll on May 22, 1958.

CHAPTER 4

Enewetak Atoll

I was getting pretty excited by this time, as can well be imagined. However, the trip to Enewetak and my participation in the atomic tests was not public knowledge, and I needed to keep any details of my participation confidential. I do not think it was particularly classified information, but there was an official desire to avoid any publicity about NRDL's nuclear weapons testing activities. I tried to keep the secret. My parents, professors, roommates, a couple of fraternity brothers, hasher friends, and a few others knew where I was going. One of my excuses for blabbing about my upcoming travel was giving a reason for missing planned events that would take place over the summer. I needed a good excuse for my roommate, Bob Shugert, who wanted me to be in his wedding, which would take place during my time away. Surely, he needed to know why I would be unable to attend. I did refrain from placing an announcement of my plans in the *San Francisco Chronicle*.

On Monday, May 18, I stopped at the lab to pick up notes and items for team members who were already at the test site. I remember that Bill Williamson (W^2 we called him), a theoretical physicist who remained behind, provided a few gifts for me to distribute. For Evan, he had a can of instant pussy with the note, "Add water and beat vigorously." Later, when we opened the can, we found finely chopped black olives. For Bill Schell and Walt Gurney, W^2 provided an empty box of condoms with a note saying, "Ok, well you couldn't use them anyway" (women were not allowed at the test site). Roger Caputi reminded me later, while writing this section, that I also carried a Billy Graham bumper sticker to place on one of the project's jeeps. I thought it was a little weird, since none of us were particularly religious. Before leaving NRDL, I picked up $140 advanced travel funds for miscellaneous expenses that I would incur during the time away.

Early in the morning, four days later, I roused Wally Anderson to drive me to Travis Air Force Base. Wally was a high school friend who was studying physics at Berkeley. He later earned a PhD and eventually found a job at the Naval Research Laboratory outside Washington, DC. His Navy career paralleled mine except he stuck more to basic research as opposed to my areas in applied research. We were fast friends and he was happy to drive me to Travis, which was about an hour to the northeast toward Sacramento, for a 7:30 a.m. check-in. I had to report to the Military Air Transportation Service (MATS): the combined military service that ferried people from the U.S. to the rest of the world. We took my '55 Austin Healey, which Wally had been instructed to place in pre-arranged storage until my return. (He did so, but I'm sure he tested its handling a bit before arriving at the garage.)

I arrived at Travis early, as instructed, and followed a long series of check-in procedures, leading from one office to another, each office telling me that I was not on the list to fly to Enewetak that day. After about an hour of shuffling from office to office, I was allowed to check my single bag containing a toothbrush, toiletries, some old clothes, and the gifts I was transporting. I was still early for my flight and decided to go to the cafeteria for my usual on-the-road donut and milk and wait for a 9:30 a.m. departure. While waiting, I decided to call another old high school friend who had joined the Air Force upon graduating and was flying for MATS out of Travis. Unfortunately, he was on a flight somewhere between Enewetak and Travis and I would miss crossing his path.

Standing in the boarding line, I noticed a tall man about my age who also seemed out of place, being dressed in civilian clothes among the military fatigues. Introducing myself and found that he was Tom

Dahlstrom, who also worked at NRDL and was traveling to join his project group at Enewetak. We boarded a military version of a Douglas Aircraft Company DC-6 that had been converted into a MATS aircraft. We sat side by side, facing backward on bucket seats in a stripped-down cabin and listened attentively to a thorough briefing on at-sea ditching and survival procedures. Finally, we took off.

The airbase runway was clear on takeoff, but we immediately plunged into a thick overcast fog layer. I recalled that the weather when Wally and I left Berkeley had been cold and damp, with the overcast occasionally touching the ground. As we climbed above the layer and headed west to sea, I said goodbye to the faint glow from the lights of San Francisco and Oakland I could make out in the distance. The fog layer remained as the plane climbed to altitude and continued to obscure the sea surface for hours. I didn't think it mattered much since there would be little to look at. It was my first flight over the ocean and when we finally escaped the coastal fog, I discovered the ever-changing and fascinating reflections from combinations of surface wave patterns and sun angles. I still become lost, fascinated by wave patterns seen in the sun's glitter, and search for the narrow "V" that follows a ship and can occasionally follow a submerged submarine.

Talking with Tom, I found out that he worked in the Radiation Physics Division with Norm Alvarez and Don Puppioni, both of whom I had met earlier at NRDL. He was doing graduate work at UCLA in physics and also worried about his final exams. He was more thoughtful than I and had arranged for a proctor through the lab to take the exams while at Enewetak. I never found out how that arrangement worked out, but it sounded better than taking all the finals at once later in the summer.

Time passed slowly, but finally we began talking about our stopover in Honolulu. It was the first time out of the country for both of us. Unlike commercial flights where the pilot announces the pending arrival, without warning a beautiful green island suddenly appeared through a break in the clouds that had begun to form. We began descending, and as the plane curved gracefully into a landing pattern, another island appeared in the distance. It was as though someone had pasted a lush, tropical photo from *National Geographic* in the window in front of us.

MATS was taking us from Travis Air Force Base to Hickam Air Force Base, Pearl Harbor, for a short stopover, then on to Kwajalein, an island somewhere just north of the equator in the western Pacific. We stepped off the plane at Hickam Air Force Base into 90 degree plus heat and humidity, a dramatic but pleasant change from Travis. It was four in the afternoon; the flight had taken about ten hours, with a three-hour time change. We retrieved our bags, changed into cooler clothing, and checked in for our next flight segment. Since we had about four hours before takeoff, we gave Hickam a quick once over and decided to hitchhike into Honolulu. Tom had heard that the Waikiki Sands Hotel was a good place to eat, and that is where we headed.

A sailor picked us up as we walked through the base guard gate onto Nimitz Highway. He dropped us near the downtown center with instructions on how to take the bus to Waikiki Beach and the hotel. I remember the Waikiki Sands Hotel restaurant as being relatively small, with appropriate South Sea decorations. Its main feature was an opening onto the beach, providing an impressive but intimate setting. In 1958, Waikiki Beach was a much smaller version of the grand tourist area it is today. Since it was early for dinner, the restaurant was nearly empty and we were ushered to a table facing the beach, surf, and setting sun.

Growing up in San Diego, I was a dedicated body surfer and took particular interest in the wave pattern before us. There were several surfers on long boards angling toward the beach on perfect, long, parallel cresting waves, unlike the crashing, shorter waves typical of much of the California coast. Every surfer seemed to be a pro, standing elegantly as though part of the heavy board for long, smooth rides. I noticed that the sky was never completely clear, and a short, sudden shower fell while we enjoyed a drink before ordering dinner. The temperature was perfect and there was a gentle breeze off the beach. I sat still for a while taking it all in and contrasting the setting with my familiar surfing area in Coronado, San Diego.

Dinner was a pleasant experience compared to the sorority meals I had served in Berkeley. We both had a good-sized beef filet cooked to order and salads from a smorgasbord table containing every vegetable and fruit I had ever seen and some I had not even heard about. It was hard to decide which items to take, and we ended up overfilling our plates and stuffing ourselves. Tom had a good appetite, which was to serve him well later at the dinner table at Enewetak.

We left before the floorshow began, to avoid the cover charge, and walked a while alternately along the beach and the adjacent street. Waikiki Beach reminded me of Palm Springs by the way the shops and hotels tightly pack both sides of the street. I mailed some postcards home to Mom and Dad, and to some friends, from the Princess Kaiulani Hotel. After a scotch and water at Trader Vic's restaurant to fortify ourselves for the long trip to come, we grabbed a bus back to Hickam. We walked into the terminal just in time to hear our names called for the flight to Kwajalein Island (Kwaj), largest of the islands that make up the atoll by that name.

Kwajalein Atoll

Kwajalein Atoll is a ring-shaped island reef tracing the rim of an ancient underwater volcano located near the middle of the Marshall Islands in the Pacific, a couple thousand miles west of Hawaii, and nearer the equator (Fig. 2). I tried to sleep during the flight, but the plane continually rattled and was alternately too hot or too cold. We landed on Kwaj just before sunup after another ten hours in the air. It is one of the largest atolls in the world and has massive coral reefs. It served as a major staging base for most of the thermonuclear weapons tests conducted by the U.S. at Enewetak and Bikini Atolls. Kwaj was the stopover for all air traffic to Enewetak and the last outpost for women participating in the weapons tests. We understood that we had to wear clothing during our stay on Kwaj. (Apparently, some of the scientists on Enewetak preferred to work in the hot sun "in a state of nature.")

The atoll is part of the Republic of the Marshall Islands. Kwaj is a national cultural heritage site for the Marshallese people of the Ralik Chain and holds an important place in Marshall Islander cosmology.

Settled by Germany in the late 1800s, the island developed thick copra plantations to produce coconut oil. After World War I, a large part of the Marshall Islands was ceded to Japan under a League of Nations agreement. The islands later became part of an outer ring of defense for Japan against rising American influence and provided them a location for a secret military buildup, thwarting the League's mandate.

After World War II, Kwajalein Atoll became a U.S. Trust Territory of the Pacific Islands, allowing the U.S. Army to build the facilities needed for nuclear weapons testing. Kwajalein Atoll also became the target site for ICBM tests launched from the West Coast of the U.S. Currently, the U.S. leases 11 of the 97 islands in the atoll to support the Ronald Reagan Ballistic Missile Defense Test Site and to assist GPS operations. The commercial firm SpaceX (Space Exploration Technologies, Corporation) has launched its Falcon rockets from one of the islands.

Since Kwajalein Atoll is about 15 degrees nearer the equator than Hawaii, I should not have been surprised about the heat and humidity we suffered when we stepped off the plane. It seemed as though someone was smothering me in a warm, wet blanket. I gasped for a minute or so, trying to acclimatize, when someone said, "Don't spit, it will raise the humidity and start raining." Tom Dahlstrom and I were dripping wet with sweat within minutes. I was hoping that Enewetak, lying further north, would not be as uncomfortable. We completed the check-in procedure and decided to spend our two-hour layover exploring the island.

Outside the terminal, it was eerily quiet for an air base, since daily activities had not yet begun. We walked away from the airstrip toward a group of low buildings. The enlisted men's barracks were simple single-story wooden structures, but the adjacent officer's quarters were newer two-story concrete buildings. A baseball field and outdoor movie theater were nearby, and there was a small park with a wooden sailboat placed on supports in its center. Palm trees were sparsely scattered throughout the park's grass and patches of sand. A small church stood nearby, with an old Japanese cannon painted white guarding its entrance.

We made our way to the eastern beach in time to see the sun appear through a thin cloud layer gracing the horizon. It was a beautiful sight, and I could feel the newborn rays of the sun begin to warm my face. I had imagined a sunrise on a tropical island would be like this. We sat down on the sand, stretched out, and not saying much, absorbed the new experience. I focused on the struggle of a small insect in the sand nearby, wanting, for a moment, to stay there forever, free from the monotony and throb of aircraft engines.

After a while, we decided to walk along the beach and back toward the airfield. Seeing the ruins of pillboxes and still-visible traces of barbed-wire fencing, I imagined what terrible battles the Marines had waged on Kwajalein. We came upon a worn signpost still supporting individual boards with fading writing, giving the mileage to different cities: Hong Kong, New York, etc. I think San Francisco was about 5,000 miles. Back at the airfield we killed time looking through some glass display cabinets filled with local sea creatures, some quite ferocious looking. There was a number of unrecognizable aircraft parked near the runway.

I began to realize that my movie-fed expectation of life on a tropical island, surrounded by beautiful native girls and low hanging fruit, was nonsense—Kwaj was the opposite end of the spectrum, where the military attempted to reproduce stateside living conditions. What would Enewetak be like? It too must be well provisioned and have some of the day-to-day leisure activities that men enjoy at home, especially when female companionship got no closer than here at Kwaj.

The plane left Kwaj about 8 a.m., following the islands in the atoll north for a while, then turning slowly to the west. Enewetak Atoll lies west and about three degrees to the north of Kwajalein Atoll—not far enough north to notice a change in the heat. I thought briefly again about how I would dread spending the summer in the oppressive humidity. Since the ocean view from high altitude was still new to me, I watched the islands pass one-by-one below for as long as possible, marveling at the beauty of the shallow underwater reefs. As the ocean turned deep blue, I settled back and waited. It seemed that only moments had passed before Enewetak Atoll came into view on the horizon as an almost unbroken rim of white sand tilting into an ellipse against the deep blue sea. The rim lay just below a horizon obscured by haze, blending it into a sea-blue sky above. Everything was speckled with cloud puffs. We landed without delay at about 10 a.m.

Enewetak Island

Although the humidity was the same as it had been on Kwaj, the change in activity was dramatic. Because it was later in the morning, everyone was at work, in a hurry, and from their faces, intent about their tasks. The Enewetak Island airstrip looked to me like what a large airbase would be during wartime (again, my only reference was WW II movies). Aircraft were taking off and landing continuously while older transports, helicopters, and Cessna LC 19 "Bird Dogs," lined up, waiting to enter the runway. There were many aircraft I could not identify. A seemingly endless number of officers in Bermuda shorts with knobby knees moved about, pursuing obviously important tasks.

Enewetak Island (Fig. 6) had been renamed Fred by the Atomic Energy Commission during the weapons test period. Some of the islands in the atoll were renamed for convenience, and to make identification and communication easier than trying to remember their native pronunciation and spelling. Enewetak Island was "Fred" and Parry Island, just north of Enewetak Island (Figs 6 and 7), became "Elmer." I was not able to find the origin of the name "Parry," which is different from the other islands that have their native names. Enewetak Island was also called "Babacoote" and Parry Island was known as "Heartstrings" and "Overbuild" to the Americans during the World War II invasion. Other islands in the Enewetak and Bikini Atolls received similar non-descriptive names. (For brevity, I will use "Enewetak" to designate the island and specify when I mean the atoll.)

The group Tom and I traveled with was ushered into a Quonset hut for roll call. Naturally, my name was not on the manifest. I watched as the others jumped into a truck and were whisked off to some restricted facility. Stranded, I spent the remainder of the morning sitting on a bench in a nearby tent while an enlisted sailor investigated the reason my name did not appear on the manifest of expected personnel.

Finally, my boss called and demanded that they immediately send me to Parry Island, "To hell with the list!" Within minutes, sailors hustled me down to the water taxi pier and bid me goodbye. Just as I got on the taxi, I remembered that I had left my military orders back in the tent. My escort assured me that they would send them to me on Parry Island aboard the next water taxi. Parry Island had been renamed "Elmer," but since its earlier name was easy to remember, everyone used its original name.

The water taxi was a small, rather ordinary passenger ferry similar to ones I rode between San Diego City and North Island, during my earlier summer employment at the Naval Air Station. The trip lasted about 15 minutes, and we passed over beautiful clear water that changed in a continuous spectral slide from light green near the shore to deep blue in the deeper channel between Enewetak and Parry.

Most of the scientific personnel were concentrated on Parry, to be close to their various projects. The island contained housing, dining, and recreation facilities, as well as a number of high-security compounds where nuclear weapon preparation, test instrumentation checkout, and data analysis took place. It also had a short runway for smaller aircraft. My workspace was located on Parry, but some NRDL projects using high-altitude air sampling instruments needed a place to work next to the longer runway and had facilities on Enewetak.

The Battles for Enewetak and Parry Islands

I had more interest in World War II battles that might have taken place on Enewetak Atoll than at Kwajalein Atoll, since I would be spending more time there and hoped to have a chance to see some of the battle sites. I had heard, of course, about some of the Pacific battles like Guadalcanal and Iwo Jima during high school, but I had no idea whether any fighting had taken place on any of the Enewetak Atoll islands.

My closest exposure to World War II was on a movie set while attending USC, which I still fondly recall. One afternoon, while lounging about the Sigma Chi house living room, one of the brothers answered a call on the house phone. He came running into the living room and shouted, "Do any of you guys want to be in the movies?" There were several of us nearby and we all shouted back, "Yes!" Who would pass up such an offer? A representative of 20th Century Fox was on the phone asking if Sigma Chi Fraternity could send over several men to be extras. The pay was $50 for a day's work as non-speaking fill-ins for scenes in the middle of filming.

We all volunteered and had to show up at 8 a.m. at the studio a couple of days later. I ended up in three scenes in *The Revolt of Mamie Stover*, starring Jane Russell as Mamie and Richard Eagan as a soldier who cared for her. I checked a DVD of the movie years later to see if I appeared in any of the three scenes I dressed for. I thought there might be a chance in one scene for a full-face frame or two, since a sailor standing next to me in a line waiting to "visit" Mamie had a couple of speaking lines. But, no. It was a short career in tinsel town and a weak exposure to what life in the Army might have been like in the Pacific campaign during World War II.

I still cannot imagine how frightening the real Pacific war must have been to a young soldier. When they reached Parry, American forces were in a "sweep-up" stage of the war in the Pacific, moving north from the Solomon Islands and the battle of Guadalcanal Island in 1942. The drive continued north through the Gilbert and Caroline Islands, with a major battle on Tarawa Atoll in November that year, on the way to Kwajalein Atoll. Truk Island in the Carolinas came under attack in February 1944, almost simultaneously with an attack on Kwajalein. The two allied forces island-hopped and left scattered, isolated Japanese forces behind in the push to the Marianas, from where the new B-29 Superfortresses could reach Tokyo.

The Japanese spread their considerable forces in the Marshall Islands unevenly over the immense area. Admiral Nimitz's carrier groups had been attacking Japanese air defenses, and he decided to establish a major base on Kwajalein Island before facing the more heavily defended islands. Fascinated by aircraft carriers, I was surprised to discover that the *USS Enterprise* (CV-6) participated in the attack on Enewetak Atoll. She was predecessor of the first nuclear carrier USS Enterprise (CVN-65). I spent two weeks aboard the CVN-65 on Yankee Station off North Vietnam in 1967, conducting radar sensor research for the Navy. Nicknamed the "Big E," "Lucky E," and "The Grey Ghost" for her survival record, CV-6 was commissioned before World War II and survived the war, along with only two other carriers.

The Americans arrived at Kwajalein Atoll late in the Pacific War on January 29, 1944.[11] Driving north from Tarawa, Kwajalein Atoll was a major steppingstone for the planned attack on the Japanese mainland. After suffering high losses at Tarawa, Americans refined their amphibious assault tactics and approached Kwajalein Island with a massive naval bombardment. Facing little resistance and outnumbering the defenders five-to-one, nearly all of the 8,000 Japanese defenders died. Allied losses were 372. The Kwajalein Island assault had gone smoothly, since the Japanese had scattered their defenses around the atoll, and there was little resistance remaining on the island. The assault force then moved west to Enewetak Atoll.

Defending the islands was difficult because of their size, limited geographical features, and long supply lines. Once on these remote islands, help was far, far away. The Japanese overextended their forces relative to the progressing American assault force that moved toward them, and they knew it. Admiral Spruance had just destroyed a major fraction of the potential relief Major General Nishida might have expected from Truk Island to the west. The Japanese were once again outnumbered five-to-one.[12]

The allies met little resistance after the naval bombardment when they took Engebi on the northern edge of Enewetak Atoll. Out of the 1,200 defenders, only 19 surrendered. Information indicated that resistance on Enewetak Island would also be light, so a light shore bombardment took place. However, the allied forces were surprised.

---

[11]   https://en.wikipedia.org/wiki/Battle_of_Kwajalein.

[12]   http://www.stamfordhistory.org/ww2_eniwetok.htm.

The Japanese were well entrenched on Enewetak Island and offered such a strong resistance that the island was not secured for five days. Thirty-seven American troops were lost compared to about 800 defenders.

Next in line, Parry Island received heavy bombarded by battleship guns from distances offshore as close as 1,500 yards. When the Marines landed on February 21, 1944, fighting was over in a day. Admiral Nimitz and the U.S. Navy had learned a lesson.

The American drive north continued into the Marianas, resulting in the capture of Saipan and Tinian Islands, 625 miles to the north. These islands became major bases for the tightening move on the Japanese mainland. Many tough battles were to come until the *Enola Gay* and two escort B-29s took off from Tinian, on August 6, 1945, for the 600-mile trip to Hiroshima. Unlike the resistance faced on Enewetak, *Enola Gay* and her scientific observation and blast measurement escorts received little attention from the Japanese. Expecting little harm from three aircraft after experiencing waves of hundreds of bombers, no defense fighters scrambled to meet the aircraft.

First Day on Parry Island

I was met by Bruce Moyer when I landed on Parry and was driven to the barracks to get settled before reporting for work. I knew Bruce as the head of the Civilian Personnel Office at NRDL, and it was odd to see him in shorts without a tie. He was always fair and personable at the lab, and we became friends while thrown together in the field over the days that followed.

Our barracks were typical Army rectangular, two-story, concrete, steel, and aluminum rectangular structures with stairs at each end. Each floor had a central hall running the building length, with aluminum partitions for rooms on each side The heads and showers were located in the middle of the building. Each room contained two or three steel-frame single beds and sometimes a bunk bed, depending on how crowded things became. The rooms also held a locker for each occupant and a table with two or three metal chairs. The floors were concrete and the sides of the building were made almost entirely of large, top-hinged aluminum panels containing windows that could open. Bruce said the large wall panels could be opened wide to reduce the overpressure from shock waves from nearby nuclear bursts. Things were going to be exciting around here!

Evan and his group (designated Project 2.3) had occupied all the available rooms on the second floor, so Bruce put me in one of the smaller first-floor rooms. I picked a bed near two smaller aluminum windows and placed my meager belongings in the locker. The bedding consisted of two sheets and a pillow. I was worried about getting cold but soon found that the temperature never dropped below 75 degrees Fahrenheit. I had a single roommate but hardly ever saw him because he worked long hours on Enewetak Island. Tom Dahlstrom had arrived earlier and joined his group (NRDL projects 5.1, 5.2, 5.3) in an adjacent building. His projects included conducting post-detonation, high-altitude radioactive air sampling measurements and required the long runway on Enewetak for the high-altitude research aircraft.

Before Bruce returned to work, he said I should walk back to the security office and be processed for a special badge that allowed me access into high-security work areas. Not all work areas were accessible—only those designated for Project 2.3. All my colleagues were at work, and I could not join them until I got the special access badge. (For example, I did not have access to the buildings preparing the nuclear devices for testing.)

I was photographed at the security office and told that I would receive a badge in two days. This would have left me alone except in the evenings and meal times for the next couple of days. As I left the security office, a clerk told me to return in a couple of hours in case it was ready sooner. It was, and I picked it up before returning to the barracks later that afternoon. (See Fig. 8 for images of the badges of all the Project 2.3 personnel at Hardtack 1.) The sigma number remaining in the lower corner of my badge indicated which buildings we could enter. The back of my badge, for some reason unknown to me at the time, also specified that I could use binoculars. (My boss knew that I would need them later.)

I used the time waiting for my badge to become familiar with the island and continue acclimatizing to the heat and humidity. I was initially annoyed with the continual sweating, even without exertion, but realized that I would hardly notice any discomfort in a few days. My first stop was a perimeter investigation of the compound area assigned to Project 2.3. There was not much to see from the outside.

High barbed-wire fencing surrounded the several small buildings that made up our compound, and civilian guards patrolled the perimeter. I would just have to wait to satisfy my curiosity about what conditions I would be working in. About 100 yards from the compound, I found a fairly well-equipped gym consisting of a weight room and a matted area for floor activities. Here I later spent many a noon hour with Evan following the instructions of Chief Lou Gomez, Evan's NRDL-assigned military assistant. Lou enjoyed physically punishing us under the guise that physical fitness training was good for the project. The sit-ups were particularly dreadful, consisting of endless upper body and leg raises until we cried uncle. Just anticipating the torture would initiate profuse sweating, and after an hour the exercise would nearly drown me.

Continuing my walk, I also discovered a small library with a solid collection of Pacific island literature, but little current information. A modern, newly constructed church that scheduled consecutive services for a number of faiths was nearby. The afternoon quickly progressed to quitting time, and I headed back to the barracks to join the others for whatever activities ensued.

What ensued was a harbinger of times to come. It was Saturday night, and a celebration of the hard work and successful data collection during *Wahoo*, the first Project 2.3 underwater detonation, was beginning. *Wahoo* had taken place two weeks earlier and had been particularly stressing on Evan and the team. They needed to relax and we all headed to Sonoma Beach. (I will describe *Wahoo* and the difficulties rearming the instrumentation array as well as *Umbrella* events in detail later.)

Sonoma Beach was the lagoon beach area where most of the instruments were prepared to go to sea. It was located near the southern end of Parry, several miles from the *Wahoo* and *Umbrella* detonation coordinates. The work area consisted of a single building with canvas sides, some concrete pads, benches with rain covers, and a sand ramp for launching floating platforms containing instruments for Project 2.3 and joint projects.

Just north of the work area, there was a large sand pile about 20 feet high, with a small structure at its base. The structure was similar to a carnival-game stand, with palm frond decorations and a serving bar across the front, with a sign above saying "Sonoma Beach" (Fig. 9). This was where Project 2.3 held numerous parties, celebrating at any opportunity or just relaxing after work. The construction and evolution of the Sonoma Beach Club (SBC) is an interesting tale I will recount later.

I recall that the evening was one of the more leisurely, laid-back parties that occurred at Sonoma Beach. It was more a quiet evening of relaxation with little drinking, some singing, and re-telling of stories about what happened during *Wahoo*. Sammy and Manny, part of the Hawaiian support personnel warmly integrated into Project 2.3 activities, played their guitars and sang native songs for us. We joined in a bonfire circle just like kids at summer camp. The evening passed quietly and people left one-by-one or in small groups until there were only a few of us left. I finally left, deciding that my first day on Parry Island had been long enough.

CHAPTER 5

Professors, Colleagues, and Characters

It was during my time on Parry that I began to understand fortunate I was to be witnessing amazing scientific and history-making events—and that during my young life, I had also been privileged to meet and interact with some extraordinary and impressive people.

As I looked back among those who contributed significantly to my participation in Operation Hardtack, I found that my journey started earlier than getting the summer job at NRDL. I include Jules Jacques, my band leader during high school, who taught me the self-discipline I needed at NRDL by making me play a solo trombone piece five times in succession without a single mistake before being allowed to even try it with band accompaniment. In addition, there was Mr. Nichols, my high school science teacher, whom I credit for changing my career direction from music to science. Both teachers stimulated my curiosity and taught me the discipline needed to earn the opportunity to participate in Hardtack I. There were also a couple of professors with whom I rarely got a chance to speak but who made memorable impressions on me far beyond their course content. Finally, there were my colleagues at NRDL, who helped mold indelible elements of my character and professional life.

Physics Professors at Berkeley

Over the years, the physics department at Berkeley rivaled other great American universities by producing an abundance of Nobel Prize Laureates. As a student, I was aware that Cal was a special place for an education in science. Finding myself involved in nuclear weapons effects research, the halls seemed to reverberate with the names Earnest Lawrence, Emilio Segrè, Glenn Seaborg, Edwin McMillan, Owen Chamberlain, Robert Oppenheimer, and Edward Teller. However, although impressive, for me these scientists were ghosts of the past (except for Teller, who occasionally gave a lecture to a lower-division physics classes) and did not affect my day-to-day lecture and study routines. Today, I do not recall the particular content of the lectures, but I do recall several professors I had (both before and after Operation Hardtack I) and some of their unusual teaching methods and comments.

Professor Leonard Loeb taught an upper-division thermodynamics course. For my curriculum, I was required to take thermodynamics in both the physics and engineering departments. Looking back, I see that it was important to study both the theoretical and applied aspects of the subject as parts of an interdisciplinary science education. Professor Leonard Loeb, a pillar of the physics department, taught me thermodynamics—the theoretical side, but in a manner that I will never forget.

What is all that scribbling on the blackboard? I thought as I entered the lecture hall and took a seat that first day of class.

A few minutes later, an elderly, grey-haired man of slight stature, wearing a dark suit, entered the room and introduced himself as Professor Loeb. With no further ado, he turned away from the rows of silent students to the blackboard, pointed toward an equation in the upper left corner of the scribbles, and began to talk about it. I don't remember the equation, but it could well have been Plank's formulation of the thermal radiation emitted from a black body, introducing the concept of energy taking on discrete levels instead of a continuous spectrum as the temperature of the body changed. That equation often dominates beginning chapters in thermodynamics textbooks.

Professor Loeb was what I would now call a Plankian theorist and experimentalist, who got his PhD at the University of Chicago under Robert Millikan and who appeared to never have fully accepted Schrödinger's wave approach to quantum mechanics. Professor Loeb had grown up in Berkeley and attended Cal through his sophomore year before moving to New York to be with his parents. He spent several years in Europe during World War I and later in America, working on his PhD, meeting many of the great physicists of the time and discussing the current quantum theories. He returned to Berkeley in 1923 as an assistant professor in the then small physics department. He was instrumental in recruiting physicists like Lawrence and Oppenheimer and setting the standards of excellence the department demanded by the time I arrived.

Week after week throughout the course, Professor Loeb talked into the blackboard and meticulously pursued a torturous path with a long pointer through the chalk-outlined regions that corralled equations inscribed just below the resolution needed for students in the back of the room to see. As I said, I do not remember details of the content, but I found the teaching method extremely bizarre for his lack of interaction with the students. But in retrospect, Professor Loeb helped me to be more self-sufficient while at Berkeley.

Professor Donald Glaser (1960 Nobel Prize Laureate for inventing the bubble chamber) walked into nuclear physics class one day near the end of the 1959 term and announced something to the effect of, "I am no longer going to teach, I am going back to school." He followed by saying that it was time for him to change direction and take up a new field! He felt he had reached a plateau of creative output in particle physics and was going to study molecular biology, believing that such a change would allow him to regain vitality in an important area of research and apply his experience in different and unique ways. He became a professor of physics and neurobiology in the Berkeley Graduate School.

I listened to him carefully and never forgot the spirit of those words. While at NRDL, I too went back to school. In my spare time, I took classes in botany, biology, bio- and organic chemistry, and radiobiology.

Although never becoming a dominant theme in my career, I now have an intense interest in neurobiology, the workings of the mind, and its impact on almost all human endeavors.

Dr. Edward Teller leaned over the lectern, hunched his shoulders, and reached out his arms. Cupping his hands, he said to the audience, "Now inside the atom you will find...." Transfixed in breathtaking silence, the students leaned forward to listen to the deep, heavily accented voice. The hall was packed, and from a position just inside a rear door, I could barely see Teller as he gave a talk on the structure of the atom to a mixture of lower-division science and non-science students. He spoke longer, but I had to leave. I was already late for a class I could not skip. He occasionally traveled from the Lawrence Livermore Laboratory to Berkeley to give these popular talks to a more general audience of non-science majors. It was the first time I saw Dr. Teller, and I will never forget how he held the audience as though in rapture while he spoke of the atom.

I did not see Dr. Teller again until much later, when I was enjoying a two-year sabbatical to the Lawrence Livermore Laboratory as head of a special studies group in the laser fusion program from the Navy laboratory in San Diego. During that sabbatical, I was also involved in the Navy's evaluation of electron-beam weapons to defend ships. At the time, charged particle beams (CPBs) were being considered for a possible U.S.-wide defense against a massive ICBM strike by the Soviet Union (the DOD called the effort the Seesaw Program). When the Seesaw Program began to fail, Dr. Teller suggested that CPBs might have a role in Navy shipboard point defense. I needed occasional visits with him to discuss his ideas.[13]

My visits were short and to the point, and I was never able to break through his formal nature and talk about other subjects. However, he left me with a clear impression of an imposing person who had such a great influence on the development of what I had seen unfold on Enewetak Atoll.

---

[13]   Personal communications with Dr. Teller during my sabbatical at Lawrence Livermore National Laboratory from the Navy, circa 1973.

There were also unusual professors with unique techniques for pounding material into their students. A mechanical engineering professor I had insisted on grading tests by subtracting wrong or missed points for a problem from the remaining correct points, resulting in painfully low test-scores. I remember getting a 15% grade on a midterm, which turned out to be a C. There was a rumor of a math professor (whom I managed to avoid) who, when a student questioned the small amount of credit he was given on a problem, stating, "It was only an addition error—all the theory is correct," the professor agreed to alter the student's overall test score. He added the score up again and got the same final number, although he had increased the credit on the problem under consideration. When questioned again by the student why his score had not increased, the professor remarked, "It's only an addition error!"

One more experience stuck in my mind over all these years. I think it might have been either Professor Chamberlain or Professor Ruderman who gave my class a midterm test problem in atomic physics that totally stumped me—and I think nearly everyone else. To the best of my recollection, the wording of the problem was, "If you are on a desert island and have only a piece of string, a ball of cotton, a cork…and one or two other common items, determine Avogadro's number." What? I didn't get very far toward the solution in the time available. I probably would never have gotten the answer given all the time in the world, and today I still can't recall the exact problem or the answer posted later outside the teaching assistant's office. However, I must have been impressed at the time to recall as much about the experience as I have. Now I know that he was trying to teach us to think, not just recall formulae and apply set problem-solving methods.

My Boss, Evan Evans.

I came to know Evan fairly well over that first year at NRDL, but it was while we were together at Enewetak that I found out just how different he was from anyone I had ever met. My parents were quiet and reserved and passed on that nature to me. Although I felt I was adventuresome during high school and college, I had little exposure to people who combined scintillating intelligence, humor, and enthusiasm with what I thought was near-insanity. Reflecting on the years at NRDL after the facility had closed, I find that Evan provided a considerable boost to what natural adventurism I possessed. Not only did he exert a great influence on my development during those years, but he also infected everyone near him with his enthusiasm and zest for life and garnered enormous respect for his intelligence and compassion.

To understand his influence on me and other project personnel involved in the Hardtack I nuclear tests, it is important to know Evan in some detail. Describing his involvement in events taking place at Enewetak is not enough. His dominating personality guided every aspect of our project's design, preparation, and execution that led to the Navy's knowledge of the effects of underwater nuclear weapons on tactical operations that still stands today. Unfortunately, my recall of the chronology of particular interactions and adventures with Evan at Hardtack I and later is vague, since I did not know at the time that I would ever want to write about them and need a diary! I describe Evan through several events about which I do remember considerable detail because of their unusual nature. He certainly did not fit the conservative descriptions of nuclear scientists.

Evan's home was the large, 1920's brown-shingle dwelling located in the Hillcrest area of Berkeley that I mentioned earlier when I first introduced him. It was nestled among well-maintained homes on tree-lined streets typical of the area. The house provided a wonderful environment for his wife Joanie, son, and two daughters. I remember Evan's library on the second floor having several large windows and many, many books. Such a home, family, and a library were what I hoped to have someday. Their lives seemed complete: Evan's mother lived in Marin County and the family maintained a home at Clearlake, north of the Bay Area, where they enjoyed outings away from Berkeley and work. I visited the Clearlake house a couple of times and witnessed a lifestyle that included family hikes, joy-filled mealtimes, and theatrical productions involving family and visitors alike.

I lived in a house above the Berkeley stadium on Mosswood Avenue with two roommates during the summer I went to Enewetak and first visited Evan at home. Single and away from my family, Evan occasionally invited me to his Hillcrest home and to parties he orchestrated during holidays. Although I drove home to Chula Vista for short visits with my parents on most holidays, I tried to schedule each trip around any events occurring at Evan's home. I remember one Christmas party in particular. My parents' quiet nature made holidays with family and friends enjoyable but hardly eventful. Social activity barely rose above the normal flow of life around the house.

In contrast, Evan's Christmas party was an event to behold, with friends, neighbors, relatives, family, some NRDL colleagues, and a hoard of children running wildly among the guests. Various guests played the piano and provided a venue for singing Christmas carols. Handel's *Messiah,* led by Sam Rainey, my radiation-field math teacher at NRDL, was a main event. There seemed to be many extroverts among the crowd, taking turns telling jokes and limericks, singing, and spinning stories. I, on the other hand, was unusually quiet, taking in this seemingly remarkable event from a position away from any particular group.

Evan was the flawless host: cajoling, "laughing and scratching" (a favorite phrase), and dominating the conversation wherever he interacted with the guests. Later during the party, he would revert to his custom of wearing his tie around his forehead. When the crowd got too noisy, he would fire a small cannon off the front porch. The party became a model for me of a perfect Christmas party.

I remember Faust, Evan's dog, which had lost one of his front legs. He was surprisingly agile, but exhibited a peculiar gyrating gate when moving about. Faust didn't seem to realize he had a handicap. Diogenes was a western screech owl (a.k.a. barn owl) Evan kept as a pet, and he had taught it to ride on Faust's back. Since I never witnessed this event, I cannot say for how long Faust allowed Diogenes to ride in such a precarious position. At the time I did not know that keeping an owl as a pet had been illegal in the U.S. since 1918, when the Migratory Bird Treaty Act passed. Looking back, feeding and cleaning up after an owl does not sound like it would be worth whatever value Diogenes provided.

I never found out how Diogenes got his name, but I see some similarities in Evan's personality and the beliefs of the Greek philosopher, Diogenes of Sinope. There may or may not have been a conscious connection in selecting the owl's name. For example, Diogenes of Sinope, 412 (or 404)-323 BCE, was highly controversial in his time and known to have humiliated Plato intellectually, publically mocked Alexander the Great (and lived), and been exiled from Sinope. Diogenes behaved erratically in public, performing such stunts as carrying a lighted lamp in daylight, claiming to look for an honest man and relentlessly debunking current social values and institutions he thought were corrupt. I think Evan admired Diogenes (the man) and practiced his own version of rebellion in society through humor and practical joking while adhering to the letter of the law and respect for rules and authority.

Evan claimed that Faust (the dog) and Diogenes (the owl) were critical participants in pagan rites he carried out in an isolated area in the Berkeley hills on clear nights during a full moon. He derived this ritual from his experience years before Operation Hardtack while participating in numerous Navy radiological surveys throughout Micronesia. Scientific teams were searching for sites for future nuclear weapons tests and monitoring radiation levels on islands where the fallout pattern from earlier tests did not behave as expected. Evan gained the appreciation of local inhabitants during these surveys. On Rongerik Atoll, he was accepted as an honorary Marshallese *ali'I* (royalty). Later, he conversed with King Iawe, then reigning monarch of the Marshallese people. As leader of many of the teams, he always insisted that the science teams follow proper native protocol and ceremony when going ashore for their surveys.

I did not know at the time, but Evan had added considerable myth and ritual gleaned from the Satanism and black magic popular interest prevalent in the Bay Area at the time, particularly in the Haight-Ashbury district of San Francisco. I thought he had learned all his mysticism from that experience in the Pacific islands. I was naïve about such matters and was willing to accept his stories without serious follow-up. However, Evan believed that he had been trapped into Christianity and seriously regretted not being eligible to become a true pagan. Although constrained by the christening his parents subjected him to, he practiced what appears as some mixture of the native islander ceremony and the Bay Area satanic magic. For example, finding a suitable "sacred" splinter from a tree hit by lightning while scouring the High Sierras, he developed a ritual that allowed him to enter the "other" world.

On a clear night during a full moon, Evan, Faust, and (perhaps a tethered) Diogenes would partake in one of the rites. The purpose of the rite was Evan's secret, as was the actual ceremony itself, except for a part he once told me. After considerable chanting, the moon would affix to the end of his staff, after which he could dash it into the ground, rendering the night fully dark. He could then enter the "other" world to continue his ceremony. I never found out what he did while in the "other" world.

Evan did not practice black magic or want anything to do with such potentially evil power, even in fun. I think he toyed with white magic (the good or natural magic causing no harm) to some degree, but it never became serious or interfered with his work or daily life. I believe his interest in paganism and white magic was driven by his curiosity and as an intellectual pursuit.

On an ordinary work morning a couple of years after Hardtack I, Evan came into my lab and asked if I wanted to go see the "taxidermist."

"Who?" I asked, continuing to work.

"The old taxidermist down on Mission Street," he replied.

"Why?" was my next response. I was busy.

"I need some bat's blood, and other stuff."

That was good enough for me. "Sure," I said, as I quickly shed my lab coat.

Evan drove, while telling me about a taxidermist he had met years before. The old man practiced a different magic and voodoo ritual than Evan and was a source for various objects and potions Evan needed for white magic rites. Evan referred to the taxidermist as "Heist." In addition to stuffing animals, Heist practiced voodoo and was currently in a contest with another believer in Los Angeles to show whose magic was more potent. We arrived in the Mission and Van Ness area and parked in front of the "Studio of Taxidermy," a small shop with a large glass window filled with birds and other small animals posed in natural settings. The address was 1791 Mission Street. I was intrigued.

We entered the shop. Evan went directly to a counter with a glass case beneath, containing a variety of unidentifiable objects. I hesitated while trying to take in the strange room and stuffed animals surrounding me before joining Evan. The shop appeared empty, so we examined the items in the case more carefully. Evan pointed out a lion's claw and some oval lapis stones among the vials and small containers holding who knows what. (I found out later that a pickled tarantula, mole hearts, and hawk eyes were also available.) Shortly, Heist appeared from a room in the rear of the shop and warmly greeted Evan.

Evan asked how he had been, and Heist said the contest with his rival in Los Angeles was not going well and he himself was feeling poorly. Apparently, Evan and Heist had earlier discussed the voodoo struggle. I was quiet as a mouse through the short discussion that followed. Heist was definitely worried.

I listened as the conversation turned to the lapis stones we saw in the glass case beneath the counter. Evan asked Heist how he used the stones. Replying, Heist said that he used them to demonstrate the location of the "third eye." He picked out a half-dollar size stone and placed it on the center of his forehead—where it stuck! He then asked me to try to remove it. Momentarily taken aback, I finally reached up to grasp the stone with my fingers. It was difficult to get a good grip, and I was somewhat hesitant to be too forceful. However, the lapis stone appeared to be firmly stuck to his skin, and I quickly gave up trying to loosen it. Heist reached up and easily removed it from his forehead. Apparently, a lapis stone affixes to the forehead in some rites where the third eye performs some function.

Finally, Evan asked Heist if he had any bat's blood, which he did. Another object Evan wanted was "out of stock." Evan asked me if I wanted anything. Seeing that I was at a loss, Heist suggested some rhinoceros horn, probably since he thought I might need it. Rhinoceros horn is wrongly believed to be an aphrodisiac by some primitive societies. Thought to be a bone or clump of compressed hair in earlier times, the horn is mostly keratin, the protein that makes up our hair and fingernails. Some think its aphrodisiac property is a result of its phallic shape and its power due to the psychological correspondence familiar in the practice of sympathetic magic. Its use in powder form as a curative might be transference from its shape, since there appears to be little chemical content of value. Today, the erroneous medicinal value has driven its value so high that poaching and killing rhinos has become a horrific international problem.

Both Evan and I purchased a slice of the horn for what must have been a considerable discount, since I carried little cash with me, and we left the shop to return to work. During the drive, Evan muttered something about the use of bat's blood in rituals for creating spells and the actual location of the third eye being somewhere around the pineal gland deep inside the brain, not on the surface of the forehead. I was not paying attention, my mind lost in thoughts about how useful the quarter-inch-thick annulus of dark horn I held in my hand would be. I decided that the horn would be most effective if I employed its psycho-magic powers by allowing the subject to rub it with her fingers while I related its primitive use.

It was in spring of 1964, that Evan told me Heist had been found dead in the rear of his shop. He speculated that Heist might have lost the competition with the Los Angeles practitioner and reminded me that he himself never practiced black magic. I still have my rhinoceros horn slice, wrapped in a napkin and stored in a box of mementos. It is dried out and cracked and I am sure it no longer possesses its once awesome power.

Taxidermist Roy Heist's shop was also a popular place to buy love potions and other items used in voodoo rites. Heist was 84 when he died. Charles Tennant, Heist's assistant, who did not know anything about the practice of voodoo, was hoping to continue selling items after

Heist's death. Tennant was quoted as saying that Heist did not believe in voodoo either; he just sold what customers wanted.[14]

Later, when the time came for my son Michael's christening, I had doubts about going through with the ceremony. This would commit his soul to Christianity and not allow him to choose a religious belief on his own in later life when he could make a mature decision.

While participating in earlier surveys in the South Pacific Islands for a suitable nuclear weapons test site, Evan became enamored with tribal beliefs to the extent that he wished to become a true pagan, not just a practitioner of their rituals. The problem was that his soul was already committed to Christianity and "not available," or contaminated to the extent that it was not acceptable to this particular pagan religion. Upon returning to the U.S., he petitioned his diocese to return his soul and remove any stigma that accompanied the christening rite. To his dismay, he found that the church did not have a procedure or counter-ritual that could undo the christening. He could be "dammed" by ritual, but not, "un-christened". In view of the preceding, all appeared lost in my concern for Michael's soul—except for one possibility.

Evan lived in Honolulu at the time, and all communication with him was by post (as it is still). I discussed Michael's problem with him and discovered that there was a pagan rite he had heard about when pursuing his effort to regain his own soul, which when conducted simultaneously with the christening would nullify the Christian procedure of capturing his soul. Evan had not had the ritual done, since he was too late for it to be effective for him, but he said he would look through his records for further information. As he remembered, I needed to continue repeating a specific native phrase during the christening ritual to counteract its effect on Michael's soul. If I could secretly manage this feat, there was a chance to please my wife and at the same time keep Michael's soul free for later commitment as he wished.

Alas, time grew near to the christening and there was still no word from Evan. Finally, a note arrived that he had not been able to find his information regarding the ritual. Michael's christening took place

---

[14]   San Francisco Chronicle, February 24, 1964.

on time and without any counter-rite placing his soul firmly with Christianity. (I recently Googled "un-christening in pagan rites" and found little information to make me believe that such a rite exists. Perhaps Evan had found a local priest on one of the islands who told him there was a rite to keep the missionaries at bay, but if so, the wording appears lost.)

NRDL Colleagues.

Although Evan possessed the dominant personality and remains the outstanding character of all those I knew at NRDL, my other colleagues provided me with a broad range of learning experiences. Sam Rainey, my older mathematician colleague and friend, had a near-photographic memory and could command any argument by recalling facts and numbers, and he helped me with complex mathematical calculations. He also continually impressed me during the late Thursday night discussions we had at the Blind Lemon in Berkeley, where Tak, Evan, and Ed Schuert, my new boss, would occasionally gather. We covered every imaginable topic but usually settled on the subject of religion, as the night grew old. Sam was a Catholic and argued that if you believed in God, Catholicism was the best option of all the extant religions. While the rest of us were skeptical and continuously attacked his position, we never seemed to make any headway against his thesis.

It was either Sam or Evan who suggested that they conduct an experiment that would provide solid evidence for or against the existence of God. Known in the corridors of NRDL as the "God Experiment," a seed-growing chamber was set up in Evan's lab. Besides the carefully controlled temperature, distilled water spray, and uniform broad-spectrum illumination, the chamber contained a slowly rotating turntable holding a uniformly mixed nutrient soil. A random seed (I have forgotten what kind) disbursing system dropped seeds on the rotating table. The only difference between the two halves of the rotating table was that one side contained soil blessed by a Catholic priest who was a friend of Sam's, and the other side contained soil that was dammed (by the same priest). The hypothesis was that the blessed soil would produce a statistically more robust crop of plants. I do not recall that the experiment was ever completed, possibly because of a decree from the NRDL commanding officer. The arguments between Sam and Evan nevertheless continued.

Bob Hammond originally worked in the Thermal Radiation Division. Since that group worked days on Enewetak, we did not hang out together much during Hardtack I. He later joined the Chemical Technology Division and became a colleague and close friend. Bob and I continued our careers at the Navy laboratory in San Diego after leaving NRDL and remain close today. I still owe him over a hundred beers at the Noncommissioned Officers (NCO) Club on Point Loma, San Diego, one for each instance I earned by forgetting to close and lock my safe or by leaving some bit of classified material on my desk after work. On such an occasion, when opening my safe in the morning, I would find the outline of Bob's hand drawn in red magic-marker on a sheet of paper—the dreaded "red hand." Although I bought him many beers at the NCO Club, I continued to fall behind over the remainder of our careers together. He has been gracious enough not to press for payment at today's civilian prices. However, he still anticipates full payment.

Aku (Walt Gurney) and Dr. Eutectic (Roger Caputi), who kept their Parry Island nicknames when returning to the laboratory, became good friends during our remaining years at NRDL and have added details for this memoir. Until 2018 when Evan and Lou passed away, Tak Shirasawa, Lou Gomez, Aku, Dr. Eutectic, and I would occasionally meet for lunch at Evan's house in Marin County, where he lived with Joanie. Dr Eutectic cooked a sumptuous Italian dish or two, I brought wine, and Lou (as he did at Enewetak) added a good restraint while we worked up an excitement about old times at NRDL. I seldom see Glynn Pence, who lives in the Sierra foothills with his wife. We remain in relatively good health for our ages and still possess the curiosity and humor that I remember from Parry Island.

For those of us from NRDL who remain in contact, Katie Young and Ann Will organize a reunion at the Basque community Center in South San Francisco every year before the Christmas holidays. About 50 NRDLers originally made up the group. We spend the time together reminiscing and telling stories about our times together. I am the youngest and continually fascinated hearing about my colleagues' experiences together during NRDL's early days. Through the years, the number of people showing up at the luncheon has slowly dwindled. This year's attendance was particularly disappointing, with fewer than half the original group showing up for one reason or another. I fear that we have only a few years left to get together.

CHAPTER 6

Bombs and BRAAA ...WOANGG... ANNNN...IONS

BRAAA...WOANGG...ANNNN...ION is the sound a very large coil spring makes when held above one's head and dropped on a concrete floor. The sound is particularly loud and disconcerting when it originates a foot from a bed where one is enjoying that luxurious dream state that occurs just before fully awakening. It may have been the dramatic interruption of a pleasant dream that made BRAAA ...WOANGG... ANNNN...IONs the "perfect" sound Evan used to "calibrate" new arrivals on Parry. Ostensibly, according to him, such a "calibration procedure" would help prepare one for the shock wave from nearby nuclear detonations. I was never convinced of the spring's purpose, and once hearing the awful noise was glad I had missed the calibration ritual. Those subject to the ritual still tremble when threatened with another exposure.

The coiled device was a spring, 8 inches in diameter and 3 feet long, rescued from an ill-conceived fallout-sampling instrument designed by one of the NRDL lab engineers who had never been in the field. Project 2.3 planned to deploy the sampling instrument in *Wahoo* and *Umbrella* tests, but once at Parry, it failed all attempts by Roger Caputi and Bill Schell to make it work. The unusual spring begged to have the scientists find it another use.

Earlier testing of the spring's response on unaware subjects provided a measure of its effectiveness. Using a standard drop height of 1.75 meters, Dick Soule and Evan carefully measured a calibree's "inches of instant elevation," or IOIE. That is, how high did he jump? During "calibration," Dr. Ed Tompkins, NRDL's associate technical director, achieved an IOIE of 3.56 inches, affirming the spring's potential utility. Fearing the spring's use on visiting dignitaries, management eventually confiscated the spring.[15]

"Bombs" in this chapter's heading refers to the nuclear detonations that were going off every couple of days (see Table 2) in the nearby atolls and served as inspiration for the day's work. Since I had arrived late in the Hardtack I test series, I'd missed many "bombs" that had been witnessed by others in my group. To them, the early morning ritual of rising to the siren, heading to the beach, and facing the burst direction during the countdown for a detonation across our atoll had become commonplace. For the short time I was involved, witnessing a nuclear detonation never became dull.

Even though Bikini Atoll lies about 200 nautical miles due east of Enewetak Atoll, I sometimes walked down to the surfside beach to witness a detonation: usually just a distant, isolated flash on the early morning horizon. Detonations across Enewetak Atoll gave an altogether different impression, since they were only 20 miles distant from our beach observation area. Since I had missed *Wahoo*, *Umbrella* was the only Hardtack I test I participated in. I describe *Umbrella* in a chapter of its own, but equivalent to an explosion of 8 KT and taking place underwater, it does not represent an Armageddon experience. Shot *Oak*, on the other hand, a 1,000 times larger airburst just 20 miles away, certainly does. (I describe *Oak* in detail in a Chapter 8.)

Waking the morning following my first day party at the Sonoma Beach Club, I could not find my security badge. Supposedly, it was required at all times, allowing no exceptions and possible return home, so I went back to the security office to get another. I was told that it happened a lot and to just hang out a few hours to see if it turned

---

15   C., Evan, private text review correspondence, November, 2011, San Raphael, CA.

up. It did later that morning after breakfast—so much for needing a badge to walk around the island. However, an ID badge and film badge dosimeter were "absolutely required" to enter the high-security work compounds. Entry beyond the high chain-link fences required not only showing your badge to the security guards but also allowing them to touch it, thereby verifying that they had actually looked at it. However, where one should clip the badge while working without the burden of clothing posed a quandary. Rumor had it that during Operation Greenhouse (1951), Evan decided to test the guard's resolve and approach the compound totally naked, clipping his ID badge on his pubic hair. The guard apparently exclaimed while pointing, "I'm not going to touch that!" Evan had to retreat and put on his shorts.

The next few days now seem to have passed without any specific memories. Perhaps because everything was so new and interesting, no single thing I saw or did stood out from another. I soon began work inside the Project 2.3 compound with Walt Gurney, checking my earlier estimates of the intensity of the gamma radiation we anticipated in instruments from *Umbrella*. The test, scheduled for June 8, was just days away. As shot day approached, I found that my primary effort was being a "Jack of all trades," assisting the others who were preparing the instrument array to be placed around *Umbrella's* surface zero.

Before discussing *Umbrella* and the long workdays I was to face afterward, it is beneficial to describe the daily schedule and living activities on Parry: the routine that made life on an isolated island tolerable for those sequestered for the entire test series. There is no chronological order of the following information I have taken from my scribbled notes.

Breakfast, Lunch, and Dinner

Between shot days requiring a before-sunrise awakening, we would sleep late, take a shower, and head to the mess hall for breakfast. There was about a three-hour window for breakfast, and you could walk in anytime during that period. Lunch and dinner came during three shifts, with each project assigned to a particular setting. Project 2.3 possessed a green tag that indicated our turn to eat. Later, Roger Caputi told me that Walt Perkins (a colleague who had returned to NRDL by the time I'd arrived) had discovered the seating color scheme ahead of time and had had fake tags made up with a white color, allowing us to eat in any shift we wanted.

Our cafeteria-style breakfast included a short-order cook who provided almost the identical array of food each day. It was like going into a restaurant and ordering anything you wanted. I alternated between pancakes or eggs, with sausage or bacon, juice, and sometimes all the above one day and cereal or French toast the next. Various juices were abundant to help keep us hydrated. Lunch offered an array of sandwiches and salads for a lighter meal and a selection of hot items, consisting of meat and vegetables, which provided a midday main meal consistent with work schedules. I thoroughly stuffed myself at breakfast and lunch and did not hold back at dinner.

Dinner was an experience I have never forgotten. Holmes and Narver Construction, Inc. (H&N), the facilities and construction contractor, treated us like kings. H&N in 1958 already had a long history of providing site support for the U.S. nuclear weapons tests in the Pacific Proving Grounds. A large Los Angeles Company, it provided almost exclusive support for developing and maintaining the huge infrastructure spread throughout the western Pacific islands. I remember it best for the food and movies we enjoyed.

Filipino cooks rotated prime rib, steak, and chicken with all the trimmings throughout the week. We were barbarians with the meat, particularly steaks and prime rib. Waiters served meat on large platters to a table of 8–10 of us. After the first platter of steaks (generally a bit overcooked) disappeared, one of us would hold up the empty platter for more. The waiter would rush over and ask how we wanted the meat cooked. Moments later, he would return, not with one piece but a pile of steaks. We would each fork off a piece and quickly down it so we could get more, ignoring vegetables for the moment. Acting as though we were starved, we would keep this up, barely speaking until exhausted.

I think Norm Alvarez ate 10 steaks one Saturday night, and Glynn Pence 13 or 14! However, they cheated by cutting out the best portion of the steak and disregarded what remained. I could not get more than two or three steaks down, not because my mother taught me to eat what was on my plate, including the veggies, but because there was always ice cream and various cakes and pies for later. Wednesday night presented a difficult choice in the contest between my eyes and my stomach. Prime rib was on the menu, along with strawberry shortcake dessert. Packed meals were also available if work kept one from going to the cafeteria. Almost everyone ate a lot but retained their original weight due to the long hours and heat. The only food I missed was real milk.

Snorkeling and the Totally Tan Club

Breakfast was usually finished by 7 a.m. when we went to work. Often, before lunch, Evan, Lou Gomez, and I would head for the gym for a short workout. Lou would put us through a severe routine of stretching, sit-ups, and leg-lifts, which I generally followed up by exercising with some of the smaller free weights. I don't recall any machines that we find in gyms today. Unfortunately, I did not adhere to Lou's routine enough to get a decent six pack during my time on the island. I was more interested in getting a serious tan. I savored the days I skipped Lou's torture and hit the beach to enhance my tan.

Having reddish hair, my skin was also sun sensitive, and I never tanned deeply during my summers on the beach in San Diego. This was the best chance I would ever have to get deeply colored. Walt Gurney had organized an informal Totally Tan Club, which some of us joined. Instead of working out with Evan and Lou, I would sometimes join Walt and just lie on the surfside beach away from the others, free of our shirts and shorts, for about 30 minutes. It took a while to tan since I could not stay long in the hot sun, but I successfully covered most of my body with a reddish-brown color of some note. I remember the short, intense squalls that would surprise us and leave us with a slight chill before warming up again. A quick shower often followed the lunch period, and on the routine days after *Umbrella*, we would work steadily until about 6 p.m.

After work, several of us would jump in a jeep (we could all use any of the assigned vehicles any time of day or night) and take off to Sonoma Beach. I would borrow some fins, a mask, and a breathing tube and take advantage of the calm, shallow lagoon. The bottom was smooth and only about 10-20 feet deep for quite a distance from shore. Glynn Pence kept our small workboat moored about 50 yards from shore to rest on when swimming and as a refuge in case of an emergency. The "hookie" was 16 feet long and powered by two 22 hp Scott Atwood outboards, giving it a top speed of about 18 knots—not enough speed for water skiing.

While snorkeling, I found complete serenity and escape from any thoughts of work or my upcoming finals. An eternity would pass while barely taking a stroke and carefully searching the bottom. There were the usual assorted remnants of human occupation of the island, but the natural beauty surrounding some the small coral heads that nearly reached the surface, about halfway between the beach and the hookie, dominated my interest. I looked in every crevice and cranny and under every rock surrounding the coral heads, playing with the myriad, brightly colored fish swimming lazily with me. In comparison, the goldfish I was familiar with were dull and uninteresting, and I wished for a better knowledge of marine life, given this opportunity.

Sometimes I would lie motionless in the quiet shallow water just off the beach and examine the small collection of shells and stones that I could reach and pick up for even closer inspection. Compared with rolling waves crashing through the shallow zone surrounding the outside of the atoll or the surf in San Diego, the quiet lagoon was almost too peaceful. The only concern I had lying there was receiving an inappropriate fish bite when I left my bathing suit on shore.

95-Cent Gin

After a swim at Sonoma Beach, we would head back to the barracks, take another shower, and gather in Evan's room for a round of drinks and a brief review of the day's activities. There were always problems to resolve and decisions to make. We reviewed the next day's activities so that everyone could start the new day with their own schedule.

Almost everyone drank gin with tonic or just on the rocks. Liquor on the island was cheap; gin was $0.95 a fifth, and a good bottle of scotch was almost unaffordable at $3.90. Every week, each person was allowed to purchase two-fifths of hard liquor and one case of beer ($3.40 each case). (I am quoting Glynn Pence's cost for scotch and beer. Somehow, my notes cite Ballantine scotch for $2.50 a fifth. Maybe Glynn was drinking Chivas Regal.) In addition, we could bring back one gallon of hard liquor to the States. I stashed some Ballantine for the trip home. Some people stored up their purchases and shipped more liquor back with radioactive material labels or other security markings, but it didn't seem to be worth the risk of discovery. The evening gatherings did not last long, and sometimes we just hung out in Evan's room until minutes before the last dinner sitting.

The liquor store was a small shack near the Officer's Club. After work, a long line would form to buy something from the wide selection of liquors, beer, and soft drinks. I found it amusing that tonics, mixes, and soft drinks cost more than many of the hard liquors. Ice, of course, was free, and we would take shovels full back to our rooms from an ice machine located in an adjacent barracks. With all the liquor available, I never saw anyone intoxicated except during the weekend parties at the Sonoma Beach Club. The penalty for intoxication during working hours was immediate banishment back to the States.

Movie Time

Since the sun set late, there was always an hour or two after dinner before it got dark enough to start the movies. Every night a different movie played, generally the same titles currently showing at home. H&N had erected a large screen with a covered projector and operator for protection from the frequent squalls. Sometimes we would arrive early and sit under the projector cover, but most of the time, we would ice up a case of beer, throw some chairs in the back of the project's 4-wheel-drive transport (4x4), and back up into the viewing area. We had the best seats in the house. I remember doing this with Norm, Tom, and Glynn once when a serious shower soaked us, chilling me to the bone, but not enough to run for cover. I guess the beer helped.

I missed quite a few movies trying to study for my final exams that had been postponed until sometime in the summer after I returned to Berkeley. I had very good intentions, but it was hard to find the time with work and all the opportunities to explore the new and unique world I found before me. I remember having difficulty concentrating while studying from *Electricity and Magnetism*, by Bleaney and Bleaney, in particular. (It is ironic that the difficult subject I struggled with was to become the focus of my work for a period later in my career.) What I did not know at the time was that every instructor who promised to give me his final exam upon my return in the summer would put me off until the end of the fall term. Upon return, I found that I would take the delayed exams along with my new class finals. I ended up taking a dozen exams during the short final period that fall semester!

Other times I missed the movies because we had to work into the evening, particularly close to detonation time. None of us cared; we needed to get everything ready, and besides, we were getting per diem: 25 percent of base salary more for being outside the U.S. and 14 hours a week overtime, whether we worked it or not. (Later, I found out that my orders had been cut for a time period just below that required to get the extra base salary for long-term travel.) H&N charged $1.50 per day for meals and lodging, which was less than per diem, and my only expenses were liquor and toiletries. I saved enough money during the time at Hardtack to buy two 20-watt Bogen amplifiers, a pair of good speakers, and a turntable to complete a stereo system for my Berkeley apartment.

After the movie, everyone usually racked out. Even though I didn't do much physical labor, it felt good to get into bed by about 11 p.m. A single sheet was enough to sleep under, even with the window open during the numerous nighttime squalls. I could reach the window when I felt the splatter that came through the window flap, but it never seemed worth the effort. The sheets were always slightly damp from the humidity anyway, and H&N picked up and returned the laundry with fresh sheets every couple of days.

Moving the Sonoma Beach Club

Getok Hill had already been the favorite relaxation site for project personnel before I arrived at Enewetak. Fortunately, Evan had earlier written a short description of Sonoma Beach and Getok Hill's history,[16] parts of which I have rewritten here from his notes and from what I can remember hearing and experiencing firsthand. How Getok Hill came about is another example of Evan's enthusiasm and unique personality making Project 2.3 successful.

Personnel on Parry enjoyed the usual assortment of bars where officers, NCOs, scientists, and support personnel naturally gathered to relax after working long hours, each bar reflecting the group's individual interests and friendships. Apparently, these locations did not allow the impromptu musical and drinking activities some Project 2.3 personnel had in mind for relaxing after a hard day's work. This led to a search for their own area where they could make as much noise as they wanted and was isolated as far as possible from the barracks area and other clubs.

A perfect site on the southern end of Parry near the heavily guarded weapons-assembly compound and coracle assembly areas fit the requirements. In the guarded compound, nuclear devices were undergoing assembly from parts shipped from the Los Alamos Scientific Laboratory (LASL) and University of California Research Laboratory (UCRL). In fun, Project 2.3 personnel would sometimes drive their

---

[16] Evans, C., Evan, "Sonoma Beach and Getok Hill," May, 1958, unpublished notes, Eniwetok.

jeep at high speed toward the armed guards standing at the entry gate, causing them to draw their weapons, just before turning away. The adjacent assembly area was where the Project 2.3 sea-going platforms holding radiation-measuring instruments were prepared.

Evan recruited the ersatz "Hawaiian Army" to construct a lean-to protecting a bar and sink, and the Sonoma Beach Club (SBC) was born. The Hawaiian Army was the primarily Hawaiian work force hired by H&N to provide construction and other support services during Hardtack I and earlier Pacific Proving Grounds weapons tests. During off hours, the Hawaiian Army seemed to have another task—requisitioning materials to construct and continually improve the SBC to satisfy Evan's whims.

A major feature of the SBC was Tiki, the project's idol, patron saint, and Polynesian deity, recognized in jest by the Hawaiian Army. Tiki was moved from its original position in Project 2.3's compound security area because Navy brass believed it would create a potentially embarrassing moment for female visitors who on rare occasions might be allowed a brief visit to the test site. I cannot describe Tiki better than how Evan described him in his notes.[17]

> Tiki was a six-foot Pandanus trunk with a gaping mouth and two immense staring eyes made of half coconuts. A three-foot slavering tongue (inner tube painted red) lolled from his drooling lips. Between his legs, two coconuts hung, above them a 2 ½-foot appendage, its tip protected from sunburn by a small coconut-frond hat. His right hand held a discrete sign reading: Island Tours–inquire within. When Tiki first appeared, some infidel set fire to his coconuts, but we hastened to make clear that this was sacrilege. Thereafter the Hawaiian Army and project members laid empty beer cans and other small votive offerings at his feet. If the offering was accepted, Tiki would sustain an erection to the delight of the faithful. If the offering was sublime, Tiki would culminate his erection by pissing all over them.

---

[17]   Evans, E.C. 2011

SBC members contributed their unconsumed weekly liquor ration to the cause, making the weekend evening sessions popular. Various musical instruments magically appeared from personal belongings, which contributed greatly to the usual singing and dancing. Steaks for barbeques procured from the mess hall by the Hawaiian Army, and marinated beginning on Wednesday, made for scrumptious feasts on Saturday night. Some weekend nights were particularly lively and extended into the late hours, making it necessary to fence a plot behind the bar as a morgue for those who fell asleep.

Not all was copacetic, however. Navy brass at Joint Task Force-7 (JTF-7) Headquarters, thinking some of us were having too much fun on off hours, decided to shut the SBC down using the excuse that a small tidal wave from the upcoming underwater *Umbrella* would swamp the bar. JTF-7 gave orders to dismantle the SBC. It appeared doomed. JTF-7 was a joint organization consisting of military and civilian personnel from various government agencies. In all, JTF-7 totaled nearly 20,000 personnel and managed in a military style that reported to the Atomic Energy Commission, Joint Chiefs of Staff and Commander-in-Chief, Pacific. JTF-7 ran every aspect of the test series, and even Evan served its wishes when he had to.

Luckily, Dick Soule provided a solution: move the bar to the top of one of the 32-foot piles of sand adjacent to the SBC used to build tidal wave protection berms. H&N had been building protective berms of sand around various exposed facilities on the lagoon side of Parry and had hauled in a number of sand piles in the process. In a flash, with help from the Hawaiian Army, the top of one of the piles of sand was flattened and the bar moved to the top. The new location became "Getok Hill."

Evan reported to JTF-7 Headquarters that the SBC was no longer in danger. However, one last problem arose when a Hawaiian Army worker in a huge cat excavator began taking sand from the bottom of Getok Hill, endangering the stability of the bar. The driver reported that he was following orders to take sand from that particular pile to make berms. Evan, speaking pidgin-Hawaiian, convinced him that he was making "lots of pilikia" (trouble) and if he would take sand from other piles, he would not anger Tiki. Word had spread that Getok Hill was a sacred Hawaiian site, making it finally safe.

A Real Bash at the SBC

The SBC (Fig. 9) and Getok Hill became our primary watering holes during my stay on the island. Thirty feet above land and another 12 feet above low water level, the hill gave us a beautiful view of the lagoon to the west and all of Parry Island to the north. Tony Abramo and others constructed a wooden ramp facing off the lagoon side with a freestanding doorway at the end. Adding a door seemed like a good idea to keep someone from accidentally stepping off the platform. One or two steps through the door and you would go tumbling down the hill onto the beach below.

With all the beer and gin that flowed through the bar, we needed an easily accessible open-air urinal with a modicum of privacy from the jeering crowd. Someone suggested that the ramp and door provided the optimum solution, the door providing some privacy, and if the ramp also served as a pissing platform, surely no one would make the mistake of falling off. I never used the facility, and all I remember hearing about its christening was Sam Rainey threatening to jump and then promptly doing so. It was reportedly not a pretty sight seeing Sam tumbling down the hill to the beach, but he fared well and returned to finish his drink and enjoy the laughter.

Preparation for a major party would start midweek, with Lou procuring steaks from H&N through a slightly devious route. Apparently, H&N would not give Lou steaks for parties outside the cafeteria. But when he brought a side of beef that he said he had procured from ship's mess, they were happy to butcher it into steaks for him. Unbeknownst to H&N, the Hawaiian Army had pilfered it from one of H&N's own meat lockers.

Covering the steaks with Lou's special marinade from Wednesday until Saturday made them tender and somehow tastier than those we got in the cafeteria. We would barbeque them and add some potato salad and bread to make a meal fit for a king, or so it seemed, due to the ambiance and abundant alcoholic beverages. Interring those who fell from excessive consumption in the "morgue" was a ritual established before I arrived. I heard tell of a whole field of heads protruding above the sand in the morgue at the end of a particularly festive evening. There may be exaggeration here, but one head always made the morgue—Bill Shell's. To hear Walt tell, it would take just two drinks to put Bill under (Fig. 10). One time, a visiting admiral became interred. Project 2.3's parties were appreciated by a widening clientele.

We all really relaxed at the larger weekend parties. After his first drink, Bill would start to hula to the music provided by the Hawaiian Army and cheers from the crowd. I guess I had too much to drink one night because I remember that I was thrown into the beach shower one night by Walt, Tom, and Glynn, and afterward walking back to the barracks and going to bed, but I was never interred!

As a rule, the drinking was well controlled by the Military Police (MP) in areas outside the SBC and in by the occupants in private rooms. The MPs were everywhere, but they gave us room for fun and relaxation. They understood that movies and good food did not make up for the isolation and pressure of the work. We policed ourselves and somehow all recovered by morning, and if we had work on Sunday, we limited our excesses the night before. Our self-imposed regimen of controlled drinking during the week and relaxation Saturday night, followed by a more leisure Sunday, helped us forget where we were. When work demanded longer hours, drinking slowed and Saturday night parties ceased.

Many celebrations held at the SBC and Getok Hill followed the solution of particularly difficult problems faced while preparing and executing *Wahoo* and *Umbrella* tests. The morgue population rose late in the evening from some of my project colleagues and associates from other projects who found Getok Hill a favorite place of retreat from work. Bill Schell's internments were memorable and after one Saturday night, he went missing Sunday morning. Somehow, he had disappeared overnight, causing concern until late in the next day when he reappeared. He had conned the crew of a mail plane to take him along on a trip to a nearby atoll, possibly Kusaie Island, and had returned with a bag of fruit and other souvenirs. He had been off-island without permission and had failed to tell any anyone, which could have led to an official inquiry.

Evan and Lou Gomez officially closed Getok Hill by themselves on a quiet evening after completing the interim report TF-7 required before they could return home. The rest of us left earlier when our tasks were complete, carrying fond memories and tales about Getok Hill for years to come.

Motor Sports

We did not always drink after work. We were given a lot of freedom on our off time when schedules were normal, i.e., when not approaching shot time, and when all preparations were proceeding well. Idle hands and inquisitive minds loose among a pleasant, protective environment lead to mischief. The MPs provided us with a protective but controlled environment with boundaries we felt needed exploring. After being on the island a while, we all became expert at driving the wide variety of vehicles the military had provided. Our favorites were jeeps and a 4x4-transport truck, which I particularly loved to drive. It was quite a change after the Austin Healy I had at home, and I took every chance possible to drive around the island.

Glynn and I liked to take off in jeeps and race around the island after dark. There were just enough open surfaces to have fun without going too fast or risking a crash. Our luck with the MP was holding until one night when returning to the barracks from the SBC we decided to give the airstrip a go. Since there was no traffic at night, and it was quite late and starlight dark, we took a couple high-speed runs up and down the small Parry Island strip. After a while, we saw headlights in the distance behind us and took them to be an MP's jeep. Not wanting to be caught, we took off toward the barracks as fast as we could go with Glynn in the lead and me right behind.

Within moments, the lights disappeared and we slowed and turned toward the barracks, congratulating ourselves on our escape. As I stepped out of the jeep, a pair of lights switched on and came rolling up behind us. Apparently, the driver had also turned off his lights and figured that we had headed back to our barracks. Caught red-handed in a serious traffic violation, we thought the worst was about to happen but instead got a verbal warning not to do it again. We had done no harm and they were considerate enough to allow us flexibility in our behavior.

Another time, after a movie, Norm Alvarez, Tom Dahlstrom, Glynn Pence, and I took the 4x4 we used to elevate our chairs to watch the movies down to one end of Parry, where one of the large piles of sand still stood. These trucks have 4-wheel drive and are virtually indestructible. We decided to try to get the 4x4 to the top of a sand pile without rolling it. Three of us got out to watch while one of us first backed off a short distance, revved the engine, and smashed into the bottom of the pile. The engine died and his turn was over. Someone else jumped in, repeated the run, and took the 4x4 a little higher up the pile. The next person took it a bit higher. When my turn came, there was a good groove in the side of the sand pile and it looked promising that I might make it to the top. I got in, put the 4x4 in low gear, and floored it. The engine maxed out in low and I shifted into second just before I reached the bottom of the pile.

The engine was screaming and all wheels churning as I hit the sand, throwing me hard toward the windshield. The truck dug in and I almost made the top before it stalled and slid back down the pile. The next try got closer to the top and the one after that got even further. I think Norm was driving when the truck went all the way to the top and stalled out, resting precariously on the frame with the rear wheels mostly free from the sand. All attempts to get it free made it list even more and we were afraid it would roll over. Horrors! Big trouble! Luckily we were a short distance from a 6x6, an even larger transport that has two rear axles. We hooked a cable on the severely tilted 4x4 and pulled it at an angle forward off the pile. We decided that was enough adventure for one night.

Tridacna Gigas for Each of Us

Most of us have seen old movies, or read of native South Pacific divers, being trapped by large "killer" clams closing their shells on a foot or hand. That species is Tridacna gigas, or Pa'ua, the Hawaiian name in popular use on Parry. The clams grow on coral heads and sometimes fall off onto the sandy bottom near the base where they can continue to become larger and larger, unconstrained by the growth of the coral. In the movies, they appear to be 4–6 feet across, but are in reality much smaller. Finding one that is 12-18 inches across could also be dangerous, if you get your fingers caught. My colleagues had already been diving and retrieved a couple of Pa'uas that measured a bit smaller. One day, Walt, Glynn, and I took the hookie out to a shallow spot on the reef between Parry and Elmer Islands to find another Pa'ua. Not spotting any sharks, we jumped in with our fins and masks.

The water was beautifully clear and unusually calm and only about 20 feet deep in an area with several coral heads. We searched for a while around their bases but did not find anything interesting. Walt already had his Pa'ua, and I think Glynn also had one. I was hoping that if we found one it would be mine. Finally, we spotted a good size Pa'ua lying about 10 feet from the base of a coral head. They are visible from some distance because their darker color contrasts against the white sand bottom.

I remember thinking the Pa'ua was almost 24 inches across its long dimension, and upon close inspection, I could see purple colored marine life growing inside its partially open shell. Since none of us were in shape for working dives at 20 feet, the first few dives were to look and decide how to get it aboard the hookie. We chose to try the shark "billy" first. The "billy" was a device recommended to gullible, newly arrived scientists by "old hands" on Parry as an effective protection against shark attacks while skin diving. The simple device consisted of a short broom handle containing multiple nails driven into one end and the nail heads cut off. A strap attached to the other end helped to keep from losing it. The old hands claimed that a quick thrust into the snoot of a curious shark would cause it to swim away and leave you alone. I think we each had one, but I now suspect that Walt and Glynn knew they did not work as claimed and were leading me on to assuage my apprehension about being in the water with sharks.

Apparently, there had been some earlier successes raising the heavy shell by thrusting the billy into the opening and, when the shell closed, pulling it aboard the boat with a line attached to its handle. I jammed the billy into the muscle, the shell closed tight, and Walt and Glynn started pulling. My Pa'ua rose two feet, then opened and fell back to the bottom. I guess it sensed the pressure change and knew it was rising. After a couple more attempts with the "billy," we gave up and decided to try another approach.

It was impossible to swim with the heavy clam to the surface, even with two of us trying. We ended up tying several lines around the shell and attaching them to a line leading up to the hookie. We took turns diving but could get only a single line partially around the shell on each dive. Walt and Glynn gave up, proclaiming that they already had a Pa'ua and I could keep trying if I wanted one. I thought I had the line tight once, but when Walt and Glynn started pulling up, it slipped off. Up and down again I went, with a gulp of air in between. I made two more attempts, but the dives were taking their toll on my endurance. I became giddy about the time I finally got some tight lines around the awkward-shaped shell. I stayed in the water, checking the lines, while the clam finally made it aboard the hookie. He was larger and heavier than the shells Walt and Glynn had already found.

Back at Sonoma Beach, we took a hacksaw blade and carefully cut between the shell halves into the muscle until we could prop them apart and finish cleaning out the interior meat. Careful cleaning allowed the muscles that control shell movement to remain intact while we placed a spacer between the two halves and bound them tightly in a partially open position. By the time we returned home from Enewetak, the muscle would be dried and the shell permanently fixed in a partially open position. As it turned out, for some reason I did not get that particular shell but one of the earlier ones that was a bit smaller. Glynn got that Pa'ua.

Killer clams taken from the lagoon were slightly radioactive, and we convinced ourselves that the fission decay rate would make them safe by the time we returned home. We stored them in a transportainer with other lab items and retrieved them back at NRDL. Cleaned and dried, the hinge attaching my shells became fragile, and although I placed stuffing inside and carefully wrapped them in an open position, the hinge broke, providing me two shell halves. For years, my Pa'ua followed me wherever I moved and still sits today on our guest room porch. It has lost its slight radioactivity and is still broken apart, but along with a 12-inch glass Japanese fishing net float I found washed ashore, my souvenirs continue to elicit pleasant memories of Walt and Glynn and our time at Hardtack 1 whenever I see them.

Today, I am much more sensitive to environmental and endangered species issues and would never move or harm such a beautiful creature.

Fishing for Manini

Evan's fascination for native culture went beyond his interest in pagan rites. He also adopted some native customs in his recreational activities while on Parry and invited me to accompany him one morning on a fishing expedition. He liked to fish with a net made for him by a Hawaiian friend who also taught him how to use it. Evan described the net to me as being hand-knotted, papaya-dyed, and fitted with lead sand-cast weights in the shape of original Polynesian-style stone weights sewn into the perimeter. When properly deployed, with one gathering of the knotted mesh over the right forearm and two gatherings over the right shoulder, a near-perfect 8-10 foot circular throw could be achieved.

The netting was very light and used only for fish no longer than 3-5 inches, not the lake and stream fish I was accustomed to from my boyhood. The perimeter also contained small pockets that opened up when the net was properly deployed. When thrown in shallow, calm water, the net would fall to the bottom, trapping any small fish in its interior. Slowly picking the net up from the center would pull the weighted perimeter inward and open the pockets, trapping the fish.

When Evan asked me to go fishing, he knew that I would mainly be watching him fish. We went down to an open beach area on the outside of the island where waves were breaking on the edge of the shallow coral reef about 100 yards from the sandy shore. Inside the larger waves breaking on the edge, a series of small knee-high waves marched in rows toward the beach, temporarily leaving calm water in between. Evan showed me how to hold the net and make a cast. After a couple of practice throws, I declined any further attempt to "fish," realizing that it takes considerable skill that I would not be able to master that morning. He replied with an appropriate Hawaiian grunt and took the net from me.

He folded the perimeter of the net into three sections and laid them over his right arm while the center of the net extended toward and over his shoulder onto his back. He bent over in a hunched form, such that the net touched his body and became integral with the dynamics of the throw. From a crouched position, he would wait for one of the small waves to reach his legs, and then scurry forward in small steps, hiding his body and legs from the fish in the turbulence beneath. I followed him on the beach a few yards away, listening to him talk Hawaiian Pidgin English to the fish. He called them manini and said there were thousands of them in the breaking waves. As much as I tried, I could not see a single fish from my position on the beach.

Evan chased a school of manini for 15-20 minutes down the beach, moving only when the small advancing waves created turbulence in the knee-deep water. I was getting tired of doing nothing and was just about to retire to the barracks when he gave a hearty grunt and threw the net. Sure enough there were several manini caught in the net pockets when he pulled it up. He returned them to the sea and started all over. I think net fishing for Evan was much like golf for others, a sport that presented a challenge and at the same time allowed considerable peace and quiet to reflect on the events that surrounded him. I left Evan alone in the marching wavelets, his mind lost in concentration and a thousand miles away.

Playing Robinson Crusoe

After *Umbrella*, our workload and schedule became almost what we would follow back at NRDL. Data reduction and report preparation allowed more time for relaxing and exploring our unique environment. Although different, even paradise can become commonplace, if not at times boring. I needed to get off-island, but there were no official work-related options. Earlier trips to adjacent islands were part of larger project plans and not available for most of us. The biological survey teams traveled to many nearby islands within the atoll and beyond where there was a possibility of radioactive fallout from the testing. Some of the other NRDL project personnel traveled by ferry to their workstations on Enewetak, but that did not satisfy my desire to explore beyond our own little island.

My memory fails about how the Robinson Crusoe adventure got started, and I have not found much help from Walt or Glynn, who were there and undoubtedly knew of my adventure. Now that I am older, it seems unlikely that I would have undertaken a trip off-island without first getting approval; however, although young, then I knew it was better to ask forgiveness than approval from Evan or other officials. The fewer people who knew what I was about to do, the better. I got up early one Saturday morning, grabbed my mask and snorkel, packed a pillowcase with fruit juice, water, and a variety of fruit at the cafeteria, and went to the helicopter pad to meet my ride. The Marine Corps aboard the CVS Boxer, Hardtack I's command ship, used Sikorsky UH-34 helicopters for project support. It was a UH-34 that I climbed aboard at about 6 a.m. that morning. We flew north over the deep channel and along the lagoon side of Japtan (Fig. 6). Beyond Japtan, the atoll begins to curve slightly northwest, displaying numerous small to very small islands barely rising above the surface out of the white skirt of sand making up the atoll's shallow rim.

Japtan was a rest and recreation site for military personnel supporting the earlier nuclear weapons test at Enewetak. It had a bar, beach, and convenient shipwreck for diving to provide relief from life aboard ship. Japtan had a reputation of being a rather rough place due to fighting among ship crews, and I never heard of any of our group needing to go there for R&R. (We had the Sonoma Beach Club for our escape.) We flew beyond Japtan, landing on a temporary metal helicopter pad on a very small island. Since the trip was so short, I later assumed that we had landed on Chinimi, or possibly Chinieero. Aniyaanii, which lies in between, does not fit the slender island shape I remember, all of them being mere postage-stamp islands, much smaller than Japtan. (The chopper was noisy and I could not hear the pilot name the island.)

I made an agreement with the pilot before leaving Parry to pick me up Sunday evening before twilight, the time not specified due to the pilot's schedule uncertainty and my decision not to bring a watch. As the helicopter faded into the horizon, I turned to survey "my island."

Fantastic, I thought. *What should I do first?*

I decided to explore the island and hooked my provision pillowcase to the trunk of a palm tree to keep it off the ground in case a curious visitor became interested in my fruit. I headed south along the beach. "Wow, I thought the island was larger than this." Quickly, the island turned east and then to the north. It appeared to be about 200' wide by 600' long, and I returned to my pillowcase within 30 minutes.

Next, I ventured inside the perimeter, walking through a relatively heavily planted coconut forest that had originally been established by the Marshall Islands' German settlers in the late 1800s. There were abundant coconuts lying on the ground, but I wanted to get one by climbing a tree, just like the native islanders. I found a tree with an extreme lean and tried to climb it hand-over-hand in a bent position, as I had seen the natives do. Lack of experience, inadequate physical conditioning, and useless getoks (flip-flops) spelled immediate failure, and I skipped any further attempts.

Walking further, I came upon a destroyed Japanese concrete bunker. Along with the beached landing craft I spotted during my trip around the island, it indicated that many, if not all, of these islands must have been occupied during the Enewetak Atoll naval campaign, probably about the time Parry Island fell in February 1944. Such a small contingent on a worthless island seemed like an unnecessary dilution of forces. As I approached the bunker, a loud clanking sound startled me. It sounded like someone hitting a metal cabinet or locker with a hard object. But I was alone on the island! Carefully, I peered in the doorway to find a large reddish crab clutching an unshelled coconut in its large pincher claw and beating it on what remained of a metal desk. It would pick the coconut up in its large claw and strike the desk. One or two hits and the coconut would slip from its grip and the crab would grab it again. A shiver ran up my back when I realized how large the creature was.

The coconut crab (Birgus latro) is the largest living land arthropod, with a heavy body, long legs, and huge powerful claws that can crack a coconut. Spread out, it can be more than two feet across. This one was quite large but apparently needed to hit the coconut on something hard in order to crack it. It seemed to be enjoying the darkened interior of the bunker and paid no attention to me. I quietly slipped away.

It was time for a swim. I grabbed my snorkel and mask and entered the water nearest my designated home near the palm tree holding my supplies. I leisurely swam to the south, intending to circle the island and end up near the shot-out landing craft. The beach was uninteresting since I had the snorkeling experience from all the beach time on Parry. The only difference I can remember was diving to the bottom to investigate a shiny object and finding a piece of a Coke bottle. Only the letters "Co" and part of the "k" were visible on the milky white glass, smoothed by spending years in the constantly shifting sand near the shore.

I found the U.S. landing craft severely rusted and eaten away by the salt and action of the surf. The thinner metal plates in the superstructure were gone, except where they attached to thicker struts. I ran my fingers over the pitted and rounded but still recognizable engine block and thought, *Before too long, the beach will take away all evidence of our presence and return the island and beach to its natural beauty.* It has been a half a century since I was there, and I would be interested to see if any part of that landing craft remains.

I was getting hungry and returned to the tree for water and something to eat. From the angle of the sun, it appeared to be near noon! What would I do next? I had explored everything on the interior of the island, and the beach had nothing more to offer. I couldn't think of anything to do. I thought, *Wow, I'm bored already and still have over twenty-four hours before the helicopter returns.* I decided to take a nap and go snorkeling again later. No luck—I never could nap in the afternoon. *I know, I'll play a chess game in my mind.* I had tried a few times at home to visualize the chessboard, but not playing often or very well, I could never maintain my concentration beyond a move or two. No luck—I still can't.

I succumbed to the ennui that settled over me and lay down under my palm. As time went by, I found I could hold detailed mental images of problems and physical objects that I was working on and had more familiarity with than a game of chess. I carefully reviewed the interim report material I was helping Evan with: the systematic process I needed to integrate the dose received from a base surge with a complex geometry. Then, I systematically designed a new metal link to solve the reoccurring breakage that forced me to shift my Austin Healy without a clutch. Finally, I thought about the various girls I had been dating, trying to decide if there was a favorite. I went on and on, until finally exhausted from all the effort, I got up. The sun was lower, and I estimated that it was 3 or 4 in the afternoon. *Still 24 hours to go!*

The afternoon wore on and I went back into the water just to lounge, facing down with my snorkel on in that peaceful dream state I had discovered earlier on Parry. I thought about where I was and if I would ever be alone in such a remote place again. What if the pilot had an accident and never showed up? For half an hour, I worked up considerable apprehension about my situation. Finally, I returned to my beach home.

I was not smart enough to take pencil and paper with me, and now find that my mind has refused to recall what I did later that afternoon, at sunset, at night, and much of Sunday before the helicopter arrived. What else was there to do except repeat what I had already done? I remember it was earlier than I expected, since the sun was still high, when I first heard the distinctive thumping sound of helicopter blades.

I have lost my boyhood desire to experience what it would be like to be stranded on a small island for any length of time. Without books or some other activity to provide mental stimulation, I wouldn't survive long. That I would soon hear the helicopter did not help, because there was no reason to create a shelter or undertake some taxing activity to alleviate the boredom. I just let myself get terribly bored. Such isolation can clearly be a form of mental torture.

CHAPTER 7

Shot *Umbrella*

Of the hundreds of U.S. nuclear weapons tests, there have been only five underwater detonations to date specifically addressing naval operations at sea: Operation Crossroads (*Baker*, 1946), Operation *Wigwam* (a single Pacific Ocean detonation about 500 miles southwest of San Diego, 1955), Operation Hardtack I (*Wahoo* and *Umbrella*, 1958), and Operation Dominic (*Swordfish*, 1962). To my knowledge, the only other country to conduct an underwater nuclear test is the Soviet Union, employing a nuclear torpedo. The first nuclear torpedo test the Soviets conducted in 1954 was a failure. A successful torpedo test took place in 1957 on the Novaya Zemlya test range, located on an archipelago north of Russia separating the Barents and Kara Seas. The Soviet torpedo immediately became operational, preceding the U.S. antisubmarine torpedo (ASTOR) by two years. U.S. submariners joked about the ASTOR, saying that it had a kill probability of two: the target submarine and the submarine that fired it, due to its use of a questionable wire guidance system instead of a proximity fuse.[18]

The work carried out by NRDL and other laboratories participating in these five underwater nuclear tests is unique. Our understanding of the use and danger of underwater nuclear weapons, whether from

---

[18] Polmar, Norman, and Kenneth Moore, *Cold War submarines: The design and construction of U.S. and Soviet submarines*, Potomac Books Inc., 1993, p.28.

war at sea or from terrorist action in ocean and coastal environments, resides in the information developed in the research conducted by these laboratories.

Two of the five underwater detonations were shallow explosions. Crossroads *Baker*, largest of the shallow-water, shallow-depth detonations, created the large above-surface event that alarmed the Navy (see Chapter 2). *Umbrella* was approximately one-third the *Baker* yield, and we knew that the above-surface event would be significantly smaller. By Hardtack I, we also knew much more about the radiological hazards involved and how to mitigate their effects.

The remaining three underwater detonations were deep bursts dedicated primarily to antisubmarine operations. *Wigwam* was an operational aircraft-delivered depth bomb known as the Mark 90 Betty (30 KT), about three times the yield of *Wahoo*. *Swordfish* was an ASROC (anti-ship rocket fired from a ship) W-44 warhead and considered to be nominally 10 KT but thought to have a yield of 26 KT.[19] These are all tactical warheads designed for use at relatively close range.

Naval warfare is tactical in nature and there is little need for high kiloton or megaton warheads. However, there may be a need for warheads larger than found in conventional airdropped or rocket delivered torpedoes, due to the size and weight restrictions dictated by the delivery platform. A 100-200 pound conventional high-explosive warhead might have limited kill probability against a high-speed, double-hull nuclear submarine. A small kiloton yield warhead as on an ASROC provides the necessary effectiveness without placing the delivery platform in serious danger (if the guidance system works).

Umbrella detonation depth and water-depth conditions were going to be physically very different from *Wahoo,* and the question for Project 2.3 was: how does the above-surface radiation hazard differ in magnitude and extent? Very little surface instrumentation had been available for *Wigwam* to support model estimates of the distribution of radioactive detonation products. In addition, the Navy canceled

---

[19]   www.nuclearweapon archive.org/USA/Tests/Dominic, 2/1/2005.

Operation Crossroads *Charlie*, after witnessing the severe radioactive fallout problems associated with *Baker*, and looked to Hardtack I to provide definitive data on the range of effectiveness and hazards their nuclear weapons offered.

I found, during my short study time at NRDL, that the phenomenology associated with both deep and shallow underwater nuclear detonations was theoretically interesting and often unintuitive. I was looking forward to *Umbrella* and getting my hands dirty with the actual fieldwork needed to verify our theories concerning the dispersion of radioactive material, which was so important to surface ship operations.

The Underwater Bubble

An underwater nuclear explosion produces a gigantic bubble of gas and radioactive material. I learned that the motion of the gas bubbles produced by underwater explosions was sometimes different, and wildly unexpected, from what I had anticipated. This is important because that motion dictates the distribution of radioactive material when it reaches the surface and how it spread over our instruments and ship platforms. (Chapter 9 provides a summary of our Hardtack I findings.) There are two depth/yield regimes for the underwater detonations of concern to the Navy: shallow explosions where the interior of the bubble vents its interior material during its first expansion, and deep explosions where the bubble migrates vertically and significantly mixes with the surrounding water before venting. The proximity of the bottom also influences the bubble motion.

Deep Underwater Nuclear Explosions. A depth charge scene I watched in a World War II submarine movie had earlier captivated my imagination and now peaked my interest in understanding what I had seen. In the movie, the explosion would produce an intense, but survivable shockwave where the submarine shook and moved on. Movie slow motion simulations captured the gas bubble produced by the miniature explosion and allowed it to expand, then collapse to a minimum and expand again, all the time rapidly moving toward the surface.

Back at the lab, I had seen research photos taken with high-speed film in a water tank, showing the bubble sometimes moving laterally, not toward the surface, and finally expending its energy pounding against the solid container wall. What was going on? Did underwater nuclear bubbles act the same way, seemingly ignoring buoyancy and move sideways? Could they also move down against buoyancy forces?

It turns out that they do not because of the depth and yield conditions available; the yield is many times that producing such bizarre bubble motions. However, the underwater bubble produced by nuclear explosion yields is subject to the same laws of physics. The gas bubble generated by a deep nuclear explosion can undergo a series of expansions and contractions on its journey toward the surface. The bubble radius, contraction period, and rate of rise are influenced by the proximity of a solid surface (such as the sea bottom or side of a container used in model explosions) and the unconstrained water surface. World War II model tank experiments performed by the Underwater Explosives Research Laboratory (UERL) showed that bubble motions shown in the movies are real for small chemical high-explosive charges.[20] (Sideways and downward bubble motion might occur for small depth charges like the World War II 30-pound hedgehog and a real submarine hull; however, I have never heard of such an incident.)

The early UERL experimental work was our "bible" at NRDL and guided my first ideas concerning nuclear underwater detonations. That work involved chemical explosives, and I suspected that condensation of the water vapor interior of nuclear bubbles might produce different results from the non-condensable constituents of UERL's chemical bubbles.

In the real world, with the relative size of a submarine hull to the much larger radius of the underwater bubble produced from a 10-30

---

20   Cole, Robert H., *Underwater Explosions*, Princeton University Press, Princeton, 1948.

KT detonation, any slight influence the hull would have on bubble motion would be irrelevant. Submarine survival depends on it being a considerable distance from the detonation. Later in my research career at NRDL, I would generate bubbles with an interior gas that condenses using energetic electric discharges and photograph their motion inside an explosion tank. The goal was to understand the bubble constituent transport mechanisms that had generated the above-surface radiation fields we measured at Hardtack 1.

Upon initiation, an underwater nuclear explosion forms a core of high-temperature radioactive material that releases radiant energy into the surrounding water. This energy is nearly all absorbed within a few feet and produces a sheath of ionized, disassociated, vaporized, and heated water constituents under extremely high pressure, which begins to expand. As the volume expands into the surrounding water, cooling occurs and a gas bubble forms, finally reaching a maximum radius that depends on the yield and explosion depth. (A short technical summary of the underwater explosion process can be found on Wikipedia.[21])

During that process, the bubble overshoots its internal equilibrium pressure radius, reaches the maximum, and begins to contract. While shrinking, it again overshoots its hydrostatic equilibrium pressure and begins to expand again (like an oscillating spring). The expansion and contraction process can happen several times before the bubble reaches the surface if the depth of the explosion is great enough for a given yield. (This simplified explanation does not cover how the upper and lower halves of the bubble behave differently due to the various buoyancy, bottom, and surface boundaries. The theory is complex.[22])

---

[21]   https://en.wikipedia.org/wiki/Underwater_explosion

[22]   After NRDL closed in 1969, a colleague of mine continued the theoretical study of underwater explosions. See Pritchett, J., "An Evaluation of Various Theoretical Models for Underwater Explosion Bubble Pulsation," JRA-TR-22-71, April 14, 1971.

The 500-foot-deep *Wahoo* (9 KT) bubble's first expansion maximum radius was about 390 feet.[23] It contracted and started moving upward due to its buoyancy but probably vented the surface late during its contraction phase. Although deeper at 650 feet, the *Swordfish* (15 KT) bubble acted similarly because the yield was larger. *Wigwam* (32 KT), detonated at 2,000 feet, which is categorized as a very deep explosion, and its bubble underwent three pulsation cycles on the way to the surface. Its initial radius was about the same as *Wahoo* due to the much higher hydrostatic pressure, even though the yield was more than three times greater. The *Wigwam* bubble reached a maximum radius of about 375 feet in 2.9 seconds. Its second bubble maximum was about 290 feet, 2.6 seconds later, followed by the final third maximum radius of about 177 feet in another 1.9 seconds.

Following detonation, the first above-surface indication is the formation of a slick caused by the shock wave interacting with surface capillary waves. A spray dome rising just above the explosion from the momentum imparted by the shock front rapidly follows the slick. When the bubble reaches the surface, it vents into the atmosphere, generating a plume containing water and its constituents in vapor and particulate form, as well as radioactive products created by the fission process, neutron activation of seawater constituents, and any nearby bottom material.

Neutrons emitted during a nuclear detonation activate various components of seawater that can cause a long-term hazard if consumed. A chlorine isotope, (Cl^{36}) created from the nucleus capturing a neutron, has a half-life of 300,000 years. Another abundant component of seawater, sodium, transmutes into Na^{24}, which has a half-life of 15 days. Many other neutron activation components are of such low abundance, or such short half-life, that they do not generate as great a hazard.

---

[23]   A very good technical description of the phenomenology associated with underwater nuclear explosions can be found in a sanitized version of; Dolan, P.J., "Capabilities of Nuclear Weapons. Part 2. Damage Criteria. Change 1. Chapter 2. Blast and Shock Phenomena. Effects manual no. 1," 1976, NTIS Order Number: AD-A955 386/8, DNA-EM-1-PT-2-CHG-1-CH2-SAN.

The *Wigwam* plume (Fig. 11) was irregular, probably due to the asymmetries associated with the multiple bubble pulses and its shape as it broached the surface. *Swordfish,* venting earlier, had a more symmetrical plume (Fig. 12), as did *Wahoo* (Fig. 13). As a plume collapses, it forms a base surge, which expands and, in *Wahoo,* engulfed the Project 2.3 instrumented ships and other platforms. I wondered if there would be a significant difference in the base surge radiation field between the deep *Wahoo* and shallow *Umbrella.*

Shallow Underwater Explosions. Crossroads *Baker* (23 KT, 90-foot depth, halfway between the surface and bottom) was an example of a very shallow explosion in which the initial gas bubble immediately vents into the atmosphere. Early time photographs of the top of *Baker's* spray dome showed a very high-temperature region indicating that the gas bubble had vented directly into the atmosphere. As the plume developed, it created a hollow column and cap that represents the quintessential mushroom shape of a nuclear explosion (Fig. 4).

Umbrella (8 KT, 175 feet deep, on the bottom) broached the surface later in the initial bubble expansion than Baker but still vented into the atmosphere, since its maximum bubble radius exceeded the explosion depth. The venting bubble material had cooled more than in *Baker* due to a combination of mixing with bottom coral and its lower yield. The *Umbrella* plume (Fig. 14) was elongated and more regular in shape, and as it fell back to the surface, it developed a base surge that had similar dynamics to *Wahoo.* One expected difference between *Wahoo* and *Umbrella* was the inclusion of additional radionuclides in the *Umbrella* base surge from neutron activation of the bottom coral.

The Base Surge and Associated Radiation Field

All solid water, water vapor, bomb fragments, fission products, and induced radionuclides from the bottom, or any unfortunate targets, fall back to the surface, generating the base surge. The early time base surge can be highly radioactive. Crossroads *Baker* had elevated 2,000,000 tons of material a mile into the air in a hollow column 2,000 feet wide and 300 feet thick.[24] Sparse instrumentation resulted in limited documentation regarding the dynamics of the falling column. Base surge and radiation field predictions for yields and depths other than *Baker* were unreliable.

However, we needed some predictions of base surge behavior and radiation field magnitude to design the Hardtack I experiments. Some theoretical work and large chemical explosive tests done by the U.S. Naval Ordnance Laboratory (NOL) provided us with estimates for base surge growth for *Wahoo* and *Umbrella*.[25] NOL results showed that some simple scaling relationships based on the *Baker* data related the maximum base surge radius to the column width as a function of the cube root of the yield. However, this work needed validation with a more rigorously instrumented experiment under real at-sea conditions.

I remember learning about the dynamics of a falling water column and the dimensions of the base surge it created from NRDL colleagues Ed Shapiro and Sam Rainey. The math they used in the models of column collapse was over my head at the time, and I concentrated on trying to calculate the gamma radiation field measured at a point in the instrument array as the base surge approached and filled the surrounding atmosphere.

At the time, we did not have the massive computational capability now available with modern supercomputers, or even the commercial PC-based programs like MATLAB. I did a lot of dose rate (radiation field intensity, R/hr) and total dose estimates using analytical functions approximating the geometry of the base surge. Sam tutored me in the use of the exponential functions I needed to formulate the field equations. Once formulated, I cranked (literally) out the answers on my Marchant calculator.

Comparing experimental data taken in the field with theoretical model calculations is typically difficult and messy because one does not

---

24 www.atomicheritage.org/history/operations-crossroads.

25 Milligan, M. and G. A. Young, *The Scaling of Base Surge Phenomena of Shallow Underwater Explosions*, NAVORD Report 2987, 1954, AD045310.

have complete control of all the variables affecting what the instruments measure. For example, each of the radioactive explosion products in the base surge has its own specific radioactive decay characteristics and must be lumped together to find a composite time-dependent energy spectrum. The time history of a radioactive decay spectrum is dependent on the particular mix of radionuclides in the contributing sources, in this case the water, free field, and surface fallout deposition. These in turn depend on how they distribute spatially during underwater and surface events. Volatile radionuclides can separate differently than others depending on how the bubble mixes them and their solubility in water. A major issue was how to extrapolate physical sample radioactivity, measured hours and days after the fission process, to the early time measurements of the radiation field made in the base surge.

The total radiation intensity at any point is dependent on the specific abundance of the detonation products (fission and induced), and attenuation and physical separation (fractionation) during propagation through the spatial water density of the base surge. In other words, the base surge rapidly loses its radioactive intensity as it expands outward, adding complexity to the estimates of the radiation field. A complete description of all the factors affecting the radiation field was daunting for me.

Geometrically, the base surge develops a roughly 120-degree backward slope front as it expands. Mathematically, closed analytical functions cannot express the resulting radiation field. Mathematically stumped, Sam Rainey showed me a clever manipulation of the base surge geometry that allowed closed integration of the functions, giving the answers we needed. I could make estimates of the radiation field level at an instant in time for an instrument at a specific distance. I made the time dependence and total dose estimates by summing the intensity at different times as the base surge approached.

However, this gave only the free field (above-surface atmospheric) component of the radiation exposing an instrument. As the base surge engulfs the instrument, radioactive material deposited on the platform holding the instrument, and radioactive material deposited and mixed in the surrounding water, also contribute to the instrument reading. I was able to play with more geometrical shapes and more exponential functions—what fun!

Umbrella Data Collection

The Umbrella Instrument Array. The data-collection plan consisted of an array of platforms and instruments placed downwind and crosswind of surface zero. Instruments aboard the platforms engulfed by the radioactive base surge would record the dose rate and total accumulated dose following both detonations. Since those early tests, the exposure units for dose (Roentgen, R) have undergone several improvements, better representing the impact of ionizing radiation on exposed material. We used the units R and R/hr for all our fieldwork, but converted to rad units when referring to human exposure effects. Figure 15 shows the instrument arrays used for planning purposes for both shots. An extracted (declassified) copy of the report is now available to the public.[26] I was fortunate to be able to use the report to refresh my memory of specific instrument descriptions and operational events that took place during my participation in *Umbrella.*

Last-minute environmental and operational conditions did not significantly alter the instrument positions shown in Figure 16. The table included shows the various instrument types and their up/downwind and crosswind distances from surface zero. *Wahoo* took place outside the atoll in very deep water, while *Umbrella* detonated on the bottom just inside the atoll lip, almost directly upwind of Ribaion Island. The final Project 2.3 target array for *Umbrella* included three target destroyers (DDs) on a downwind leg and a Navy barge upwind, to map the radiation exposure at various deck locations.

---

[26]   Evans, E.C., and T.H. Shirasawa, *OPERATION HARDTACK, Project 2.3–Characteristics of the Radioactive Cloud from Underwater Bursts,"* Naval Radiological Defense Laboratory, WT-1621, 15 January 1962, SECRET RESTRICTED DATA. Extracted version of WT-1621 (EX), DNA, AD-A995-467, 1 September 1985. Approved for public release; distribution is unlimited. Prepared for Defense Nuclear Agency.

Instrumentation. We used three major instruments to provide data to verify theories describing the radioactive field and the total dose received as a function of distance from the explosion. Cost limited the number of more sophisticated instruments, so the array contained a number of simple film packs, like those used to monitor the gamma exposure we received on Parry or at NRDL.

Circles in Figure 15 show the positions of floating, moored platforms, coracles (small boats) that carried the expensive gamma-intensity-time recorder (GITR), and incremental fallout collector (IFC), a shock-mounted recorder, and film packs. Coracles had a flattened hemispherical bottom with a flat top that held the exposed instruments (Fig. 16). The coracle was circular to match the geometry of the models used to estimate the radiation intensity contribution from deck fallout and that deposited in the water. NRDL engineers designed coracles to withstand high overpressures and minimize shock pressure impact on the instruments. The platforms carried GITRs that could measure both low- and high-intensity airborne radiation and underwater radiation with a 4ϖ field-of-view (all directions up and down).

GITRs recorded data for up to 60 hours on magnetic tapes, which Walt Gurney, one of the project's electrical engineers, later read out in our compound on Parry. I remember him struggling at times with the data tapes, trying to determine the time history of the radiation field.

The IFC consisted of a stack of fallout collection trays, each tray exposed for 1 minute to the atmosphere before being stored within the instrument case by an escalator mechanism. Film packs (FPs) placed throughout the instrument array augmented the total dose measurements obtained from the GITRs. Target ships carried several FPs, and each coracle carried two: one on a tripod, 3 feet above the deck, and another trailing in the water alongside. Small buoys that could be either free-floating or moored by a small anchor also carried FPs. The free-floating FPs became my primary instrument of interest preparing for and during *Umbrella*.

Preparing for Shot *Umbrella*

There were three buildings assigned to Project 2.3 within the high-security compound area I described earlier. In addition, the Thermal Radiation Branch commanded a well air-conditioned trailer where Tom Dahlstrom (my traveling partner) and Norm Alvarez worked. One building served as headquarters for Evan, Lou, and visiting NRDL managers. Roger Caputi and Bill Schell analyzed IFC samples in another building designed for radiochemistry. Walt, a.k.a. the "GITR data master," worked in a third building, where my desk was located.

Our division head, Dr. Ed Tompkins, spent a lot of time with Roger and Bill but also roamed about interacting with everyone. Lance Egeberg and Glynn Pence worked with field instrumentation located at Sonoma Beach. Others shown in the Project 2.3 personnel list (Fig. 8) supported their specific work areas in the compound or at Sonoma Beach. The compound also contained a maze of buildings housing military support groups. I never did learn my way to a specific support desk without asking directions. At night, the entire compound area was floodlit and sometimes seemed even more active than during the day.

A concrete blockhouse contained a new IBM 704 computer, which was better than the Burroughs we had at NRDL. I often needed to borrow a set of numerical tables they had, but I also liked to go there since our air conditioning barely kept the ambient temperature at bay. I initially worked in Walt's building, checking the estimates of the dose rate and total dose those radiometers and dosimeters would receive. Later, I moved to Evan's building to work on report preparation.

Participating in *Umbrella*, where there is only one chance to get everything correct, was unlike anything I had ever done before. Back in the lab at Cal, I had just followed instructions that specified an experiment's physical setup, collection procedures, and data analysis techniques. There, taking data repeatedly can account for errors, and any major problem can be corrected by starting over. *Umbrella* for us was an expensive, one-time-only event operating in a carefully timed sequence to collect the data required. Helping prepare for *Umbrella* and the massive orchestrated data-collection process was a lesson few of my

Berkeley classmates would ever get an opportunity to experience. What I learned from the complex design of this experiment was extremely valuable and served me well throughout my career, helping to distinguish me from many of my professional colleagues.

Wahoo, although successfully providing a great amount of the data, was fraught with problems. The most serious for Project 2.3 was an error made by Edgerton, Germeshaussen, and Greer, the company providing arming signals for instruments already deployed in the array. On May 15 (the day before shot day), an accidental radio signal triggered the array, starting all the GITRs, IFCs, and other instruments that were following a timed operation. The instruments would have finished operating before *Wahoo* detonated, destroying Project 2.3's entire data-collection effort. It was only through a herculean effort by project personnel and others working through the night that the team managed to rearm most of the coracles and shipboard instruments. That accident was probably why my boss called for additional assistance.

Since *Wahoo* was in deep water, mooring the coracles to withstand the higher sea state outside the atoll, along with the shock and hydrodynamic abuse, was challenging, and several moorings failed, allowing the instruments to drift out of their planned positions. In addition, some instruments did not receive the arming signal and there were delays in their recovery due to a communication mix-up. I learned never to expect even close to 100% data-collection success from large, complex field experiments and to design such data-collection experiments accordingly.

(For convenience and clarity in describing field events, I will use the military nomenclature for event time that standardized communications among test participants: D refers to days, H hours, M minutes, and S seconds. Following each letter, a plus or minus number indicates the days, hours, minutes, and seconds relative to the scheduled detonation time for an event. For example, H+1 designates 1 hour after detonation, H-1 designates 1 hour before detonation. S+10, denotes 10 seconds after burst, and D-2 designates two days before detonation. The military used Greenwich Mean Time (GMT) designations for all communications.

However, I use local time, not GMT to describe our activities on Parry. Enewetak is 12 hours ahead of GMT.)

As the *Umbrella* countdown approached, my tasks moved from our compound to the field. Activity increased on May 27, beginning with the deployment of deep moorings located outside the atoll. By May 31, we completed all coracle moorings except for those located on the atoll rim. Pre-armed coracle attachment to the moorings began June 3. This time, the coracles had a lanyard to arm the instruments just before shot time, in case another arming-signal error occurred. While the last of the coracle moorings being set, on June 5, I began helping Glynn place the moored FPs inside the lagoon from aboard the air vehicle rescue (AVR) support boat. An AVR is an Air Force crash rescue boat developed during World War II for saving downed aviators. It was about 85 feet long, but relatively narrow in beam—and to my eye unstable in a heavy sea.

I was aboard the AVR for two days in a row, along with Glynn and Tak. The first day we started early and I ate a particularly heavy breakfast, thinking that our box lunches might not be enough to last the day. The trip from Parry to the array was horrible, since we traveled perpendicular to the sea and the AVR rolled and twisted to the extreme. I had little experience being on the ocean, except in the surf in San Diego, and did not know that I would be severely subject to motion sickness. By the time we reached the array, I was sicker than a dog, already heaving my guts out. However, I was the new guy and could not allow a bad first impression. Besides, there was no way to escape and I might as well work, sick or not.

Sitting at the stern, Glynn threw out the FP mooring anchor while I kept the lines untangled as the anchor deployed. Glynn next threw in the float holding the film pack. Although the final report describes only one basic design consisting of a 3'x3' Styrofoam float trailing a smaller Styrofoam float containing the film pack, there was another moored type of FP deployed later that I had a part in designing. As the seemingly yearlong day progressed, more FPs went into the water, and somehow I survived. The trip back to Parry took forever. When we docked, I staggered to bed.

The next morning, I did not eat more than a few bites of bacon and eggs, believing that a little grease helped maintain the stomach through seasickness. Bad idea! I still suffered all day long and felt weaker. For a while, I wanted to die and thought of ending it all by jumping into a school of small sharks we spotted. There was no escape from the engine exhaust, and the AVR's twisting motion was too much to endure. Tak gave me some pills but they did not help much and made me sleepy. Somehow, I managed through my last day aboard the AVR.

However, this ordeal was not over. We had to verify that the moorings were holding and that the moored FPs were still in place. On D-2, Walt and I climbed aboard a small single-engine aircraft (an LC-20, I believe) to fly over the array and check whether or not the moored FPs were still in their positions. Since I had celebrated my survival deploying them from the AVR the day before, I had a slight headache, and my stomach was still a bit weak when I climbed in the plane. Normally there would be the pilot and Walt with binoculars in the front seats, and I would be alone in the back with a map of their moored positions, directing and recording Walt's observations. However, at the last minute, an Air Force colonel wanted to come along for the ride and jumped into the seat behind the pilot. Up we went.

I was having a good time on the way to the array. The air was calm and the view of the water captivating; I watched the coral heads pass underneath and even spotted a couple of large sharks. When we got to the array, the pilot started a back and forth banking pattern so Walt could get a more direct look down on the FP surface floats. Back and forth, back and forth we went, as Walt looked for the FPs. Walt was having trouble finding *any* moored FPs, and I was getting sick!

The colonel could not have cared less. He was just enjoying the scenery; the plane was noisy and he did not tune into the problems we were having. I was feeling worse and worse, and Walt kept asking the pilot to repeat the pattern for a better look. This did not go on for long before I heaved up a bit of my breakfast. I clamped my hand over my mouth and looked to open the back window. There was no latch—it didn't open! I looked for a barf bag. There was none. Up came some more. I swallowed, wiping my mouth. No one noticed and we kept flying. I picked up a small tube and funnel attached to the back of Walt's seat and motioned my Air Force companion that I was sick. He finally got the message and motioned that I should not use that tube for the purpose I intended.

On and on this went. Up-chuck and swallow—over and over—until Walt motioned to the pilot that we were finished and could return to Parry. When we landed, I was a mess and immediately heaved everything on the ground alongside the plane. I revived before long only to learn that most of the moored FPs we had deployed earlier were missing.

Panic ensued. A wider survey showed that they were not washing up on the atoll islands in the array as the current and wind vectors would have directed. The moored FP floats were nowhere in sight. We surmised the Styrofoam floats were breaking their cable connection to the anchor but still somehow not washing ashore. Were the fish eating the Styrofoam? Evan proposed making new Styrofoam floats with better anchor connections. I disagreed, arguing that it would take too long to make enough new floats and get them deployed in the time remaining before we needed to vacate the area. It seemed to me that a coat of paint would keep plywood floats from absorbing water for the time needed. Evan resolved the discussion: we split up, each pursuing his own solution.

I don't remember whom Evan told to execute his idea, but I was put in charge of mine, making and painting a bunch of plywood floats to be rigged and readied for deployment. I needed a team to help but remember only that I commandeered Bruce Moyer for the job. Bruce just happened to be standing nearby when the decision was made on how to proceed, and I called him over. After I told (not asked) him to grab a broom and some paint, I felt a little funny—not the ha-ha kind of funny. I guess I was feeling proud and maybe a little pushy because Bruce was the NRDL personnel officer, a GS-14 or 15. I was a lowly GS-5, and he was at Hardtack I as part of the management team. It works that way in the field. Everyone pitches in and becomes "hands and feet" when there is an emergency.

Bruce and I worked side by side, along with a couple of others recruited for the job, to fabricate and paint some floats and get them down to Sonoma Beach for deployment the next day. As it turned out, both types of floats worked, although I think I did lose a couple and all of Evan's floats survived. Following the timing signal test on D-1, the team armed all except two coracles by lanyard within a couple of hours. They then recovered coracle instruments that had started while undergoing deployment, returning them to Sonoma Beach. Rearmed, they repositioned them the next morning. This was possible because *Umbrella's* schedule, originally planned for June 8, slipped a day due to a number of delays unrelated to Project 2.3. Detonation time was rescheduled for 1115 on June 9. We were ready.

Umbrella D-0

We were up early and excited about whatever the coming day would bring. Everyone had duties for final preparation. The two errant coracles had been redeployed on their moorings overnight, and deployment of the free-floating FPs had begun. Marine Corps helicopters tracked by radar from the USS Boxer deployed free-floating FPs, which increased the spatial density of the accumulated radiation dose data. I was part of instrument-recovery operations, which would begin when we got a radio signal moments after the base surge subsided.

At H-1, control of the countdown transferred to the USS Boxer, where Evan and Tak coordinated with Navy operations and directed Project 2.3 instrument recovery. Due to Evan's reputation regarding a dress code while on Parry, JTF-7 made a special request that he come aboard the USS Boxer fully and properly dressed, which he did. Project 2.3 had two recovery boat teams standing by in case there were any problems with the helicopter recovery operations, especially if a coracle broke loose and drifted on the reef. Each team consisted of a landing craft, utility (LCU), that had carried a smaller water-land DUKW out to the site from Parry, and a landing craft, mechanized (LCM), with a crane to help get the coracles and FPs aboard.

Marine Corps landing craft are of various sizes and function. The largest, an LCU, is about 130 feet long and used for carrying vehicles ashore from the deep-water ships. An LCM, is half the size and primarily used to carry jeeps and troops. DUKW is not an acronym but a collection of letters that phonetically identify the vehicle. These platforms were invaluable throughout the Pacific weapons tests.

I was technical director for one of the DUKWs, and my job was to maintain communication with Evan aboard the USS Boxer and be prepared to help recover FPs as he directed after the base surge subsided—and keep the DUKW away from any serious radiation field. We arrived at a holding position upwind of surface zero, well out of range of any possible base surge, at about H-2. Since the detonation would take place underwater and the initial burst of gamma rays are quickly absorbed as they travel through the surrounding water and atmosphere, we were not in danger of receiving a dose from either the prompt or the later free-field radiation. If we accidentally entered a patch of water from the base surge fallout that was highly radioactive, however, we could be in danger. We understood the level of possible danger (some of my earlier radiation field calculations), and unlike some military personnel who had received significant exposures during the Operation Crossroads *Baker* detonation, we understood the severe danger associated with inhaling radioactive particulates so soon after detonation.

The DUKW crew consisted of three sailors who were responsible for operating the DUKW and responding to directions from Task Group 7.3, Combat Information Center, aboard the Boxer. My directions throughout the event came from Evan. We wore light clothing fully covering our arms and legs, hats for additional cover, and simple masks to limit breathing any airborne aerosols. I had two Geiger counters for monitoring the air and water around the DUKW (one as a spare) to help avoid areas of high radioactivity. I considered radiation levels over 10 R/hr to be hot enough to avoid entering, even for a limited time. The thought of stalling the DUKW in a hot pool of water crossed my mind. Caught in that radiation field, if the DUKW stalled for 30 minutes, it could be enough to send me back to NRDL—or worse—for treatment.

Time wore on as we watched the last-minute placement of free-floating FPs by the Marine Corps helicopters. About H-1, all activity within the array ceased and we waited. I remember there was little talk, each of us probably thinking about what we were about to witness from such close range. The tension I felt was greater than watching a high-yield burst from Parry, 20 miles across the atoll. I felt both unease and excitement at the prospect of being within a potentially vulnerable distance from a nuclear detonation! Time dragged in the stifling heat and calm. Someone suggested we shut down the DUKW engines since there would be at least a 20-30-minute delay after the base surge subsided before we got orders to begin recovery operations. All the time our radios were monitoring the countdown as the timing sequence fell: 30 minutes, 15 minutes, 10, 9..., 1 minute, 30 seconds, 5, 4, 3, 2, 1, fire.

***

From my position in the DUKW, I did not see the blue subsurface flash that (in theory) started at about 0.001 seconds after detonation and continued for about 0.01 seconds.[27] Nor did I see the white circular patch with a dark fringe that followed and extended out to a radius on the surface of about 2,200 feet, until it was overtaken at 0.5 seconds by the forming spray dome annulus. The spray dome annulus would have formed from the gas bubble, then started to collapse inward and, by S+1 merged with an inner solid area, forming a solid white patch on the surface with a radius of approximately 1,800 feet.

What I actually saw was the forming of the bell-shaped spray dome that heaved the surface upward, beginning about 0.1 seconds after detonation. Within 5 seconds, the plume reached 3,500 feet, and a maximum height at S+35 of 5,800 feet (Fig. 14). To me, the plume angle was like looking at a 100-foot tree from a position about 200 feet away—not an Armageddon, but impressive because I knew that I was only a couple of miles away.

---

[27] *Technical Summary of Military Effects Programs 1-9, Operation Hardtack Preliminary Report*, DASA ITR-1660, Sandia Base, NM, 1959.

I watched the plume as it began to collapse and fall. I thought of the tabletop model of water columns I had seen photographs of at the lab, made earlier to study the hydrodynamics of falling fluids. They were grossly different: the miniature model columns collapse rapidly, whereas the huge plume before me fell in slow motion. After about 13 seconds, an expanding annulus formed at the base of the plume, covering much of our instrument array. By S+42, the leading edge had traveled 5,000 feet downwind and 3,400 feet upwind toward the DUKW. For the time between S+20 and S+40, the average radial crosswind velocity (not influenced by the wind) was about 60 miles per hour. By M+7, the base surge energy had waned, and dynamic expansion had ceased at a radius of about 9,700 feet. The maximum height of the base surge was about 1,850 feet at S+75.

Most of the denser portion of the plume fell back to the surface nearer surface zero instead of becoming part of the base surge. This created an energetic pool of turbulent water that brought up bottom material and expanded outward under the base surge. Eventually, the base surge became a slowly dispersing cloud, leaving a plume fallout mist that was smaller but potentially more lethal. A white pool remained at surface zero with a radius of about 4,000 feet after M+25, when the last photo of *Umbrella* was taken.

The surface waves generated throughout the lagoon were fascinating. After the first surge produced from the expanding bubble, they became a series of decaying amplitude oscillations due to the constraining water depth and limited volume of water contained within the lagoon. I guess I was excited about watching the developing base surge because I do not remember experiencing any surface wave action from the detonation. When the bottom becomes shallower approaching land, the smaller amplitude lagoon waves can crest and cause damage to shoreline structures. At best, the DUKW might have rolled a bit with passing swells from the blast. On Mui Island, about 1 ½ miles from surface zero, the first wave arrived at about S+100 and had an amplitude of almost five feet. Successive smaller and smaller waves continued to arrive for two hours, demonstrating a "ringing" effect in the lagoon, created by the surrounding atoll reef.

It was time to go to work. Anticipating some commands to move within minutes, we tried to start the DUKW engines. No luck—the batteries were dead! Frustrated, I radioed Evan the problem so he knew he could not depend upon any help from us. The DUKW crew worked trying to get the engines started but to no avail, and we sat in position and watched the entire recovery operation unfold before us. Help came, but not in time to participate in recovery operations. Luckily, we had a small role and did not impede recovery activities.

At M+30, two Marine Corps helicopters under radar tracking from the USS Boxer began picking up the free-floating FPs that had been deployed outside the lagoon in deep water, their pickup positions recorded by the carrier radar. All FP recovery operations moved inside the lagoon by H+1.5. Concurrently, the radioactive samples collected by instruments aboard the ships in the array were recovered and returned to Parry and made ready for the scheduled H+6 flyaway back to NRDL for processing. Recovery of coracles outside the lagoon began at H+3.5 and all but two that were located on the reef, were recovered by H+7 by the LCU and LCM recovery teams (except for my DUKW!) and the AVR. The reef coracles were recovered on D+1. By 1430 that day, all IFC trays had been prepared to meet another air shipment to NRDL for analysis. By D+5, the lagoon had been cleared of all moorings, and equipment was ready for shipment back to NRDL.

I was bummed! It took most of the afternoon to get back to Parry. I had a late dinner, while some of the group still worked. I do not remember where my boss was, but we were all happy that things went so well in comparison to *Wahoo*. I was anticipating there would be a massive amount of data to analyze and looked forward to getting started to salve my disappointment in missing the recovery action.

CHAPTER 8

Countdown to Armageddon

Parry Island, Enewetak Lagoon in the Northwest Pacific, 1930 hours (GMT), 28 June 1958
"Ten seconds to detonation," the voice on the loudspeaker announced. "9, 8, 7, 6, 5, 4, 3, 2, 1, Fire!"

…

…

"JESUS, it's bright—and it's getting hot!" I exclaimed.

…

They must have made a mistake, I thought.
Oak is going over 10 megatons!
I should start counting so I can estimate the yield.
One thousand one.
One thousand two.
One thousand thr—
Damn, I didn't start soon enough. If I go beyond ten, what difference will it make? WE'LL ALL FRY!
Beginning to panic, I slowly turned sideways to expose a different side of my clothing to the fireball.

***

Trying to recall, after more than 50 years, the details of Shot *Oak* for this memoir, I found that I was able to reconstruct some events with unusual clarity. With other events, only the general timeline of the phenomena unleashed after the instant of the *Oak* detonation are available from my memory and notes. I have relied heavily upon my colleagues for help to fill in what happened that day on Sonoma Beach.

My narrative follows our activities before the *Oak* detonation and our reactions to what was happening around us, interwoven with short quantitative descriptions of the physical processes taking place following the initial flash of light. Since none of us could directly sense the temperature of the fireball, shockwave pressure, mushroom-cloud growth, and other physical phenomena that followed, I have relied on information from *The Effects of Nuclear Weapons* to help characterize the physical forces we felt.[28]

June 29, 1958, began normally enough; however, we all knew that the day was going to be different. I woke about 0600 as usual, showered, and went to the mess hall for breakfast with several of the others. We talked about the test—named *Oak*—it would have a yield of 7.5 MT, almost 1,000 times larger than *Umbrella* and over 500 times that of Hiroshima's *Little Boy*. It would detonate across the atoll on the reef just south of Bokoluo Island,[29] about 20 miles away (*Oak* was followed

---

[28] At NRDL before Operation Hardtack I, my primary reference for technical details of the phenomena associated with an atomic weapon detonation was Hirschfelder, J.O., et al., ed., *The Effects of Atomic Weapons*, 1950. This summary volume was updated by Gladstone, S., editor, *The Effects of Nuclear Weapons, 1962,* and included a circular slide rule (Nuclear Bomb Effects Computer #1) that gave numerical estimates for a variety of thermal, shock wave, and nuclear radiation exposure effects and the resulting damage from both atomic and thermonuclear weapons. Later versions of the computer are available based on data that has been redacted. I have employed my old computer in this memoir to represent the information I had available at the time (https://calculating. wordpress.com/2016/02/03/the-nuclear-bomb-effects-computer-versions-1-2-3, accessed 9/29/2018.) Additional information is now abundantly available on the web in unclassified (redacted) research documents from Wikipedia and U.S. navy and national laboratory publications.

[29] http://nuclearweaponarchive.org/USA/Tests/Hardtack1.html.

by *Hickory*, a small 14 KT detonation several hours later at Bikini Atoll). *Walnut*, my largest detonation so far, had taken place across the lagoon on top of a barge. It had been impressive enough, delivering 1.5 MT, but LASL predicted *Oak's* yield as five times larger. Compared to other Enewetak detonations and the high-altitude tests held at Johnston Island, *Umbrella* was a wimp. Most of the detonations I had witnessed were in the 50–500 KT range.

Finally, the siren sounded and we walked down to the beach, still discussing what we might see. We had calculated experiencing a significant thermal pulse from *Oak* and followed the official instructions to avoid having any exposed bare skin by wearing long-sleeved shirts and trousers made of light cotton. In addition, Tom Dahlstrom and I had fashioned aluminum foil helmets to wear over our heads. Most of us had some form of high-density goggles to protect our eyes while others used damp towels to cover their heads and eyes. Officially, we should not look at the fireball for at least 30 seconds after detonation. Sure, how bad could it be? Still, since the yield was so high, some concern overlay my excitement as we approached the beach.

We took up positions above the high tide line half an hour after sunrise. *Oak* would detonate in about 30 minutes at 0730, so we mingled with others from various projects to get their thoughts about what we would see. Some of the scientists participating in Hardtack 1 had seen experimental thermonuclear detonations at earlier test series, and I was disappointed not to find one who had a close-in experience to share. Someone parked our 4x4 at the crest of the shallow beach, as high as possible from the waterline. The crowd was solemn, but there were still one or two who were joking about what might happen to us. I thought about the cables H&N had installed, anchoring the open-sided barracks and other buildings to keep them from collapsing from the shock wave. This was done specifically in preparation for *Oak*; something special was about to happen.

When the countdown from the loudspeaker reached five minutes, some of us began taking places on the ground facing away from surface zero. The official instructions were to sit with our backs to the blast and place our heads on our knees with damp towels over our heads and eyes, if you did not have high-density goggles. We knew that it would be a good idea to sit on the sand when the shock wave arrived, and nearly everyone did. However, for some reason I do not remember, Tom Dahlstrom and I stood facing away from the blast direction. Maybe we knew that the shock wave would take some time to reach us, giving time to react. It was the thermal pulse and prospect of getting a severe burn that we feared most. Normally the thermal exposure from lower-yield airbursts across the lagoon was not a problem, and for *Umbrella*, the water surrounding the detonation made a perfect radiation shield. For detonations at distant Bikini Atoll, we were not required to gather at the beach.

We did not know much about the nuclear devices themselves, since there was extreme need-to-know security around the weapons-assembly compound and we did not mix with the Los Alamos Scientific Laboratory (LASL) and Lawrence Livermore Laboratory personnel. Even back at NRDL, we had little contact with the weapons design work going on at Livermore and the Berkeley Radiation Laboratory. Later, I learned that the *Oak* device was a prototype of the LASL TX-56 family of devices and was to become the W/Mk-53 warhead deployed on the Titan II missile and the Mk-53 air-delivered bomb. Their operational yields were about 9 MT. This basic design remained current until 1997 and was the oldest and largest yield thermonuclear device in the U.S. arsenal. The *Oak* prototype device was large, over 36 inches in diameter and 100 inches long, and weighed approximately three tons.[2] No wonder it was placed on a barge.

There had been detonations during previous test operations in which the actual yield was significantly larger than the predicted yield (some also "fizzled" or achieved lower than predicted yields). Many of these earlier research devices were dedicated to perfecting large thermonuclear explosions, which made yield predictions more difficult. The weaponized warheads that were common in the Hardtack I series were, in theory, better behaved. Perhaps my concern approaching the beach was unwarranted, but I felt that mistakes were still possible while testing the more weaponized versions. I was familiar with the case of the

Lucky Dragon, which provides a chilling story of what might go wrong during a test, regardless of the precautions taken.

Castle Bravo and the Lucky Dragon

Talk about mistakes! Many planning and operational mistakes occurred during Operation Castle *Bravo* (1954), leading to acrimonious exchanges between the U.S. and Japan. Besides the political strain between the two countries, the mistakes also resulted in horrific, long-term radiation damage to the Micronesians living on the atolls to the east of Bikini Atoll.

The most publicized disaster from Castle *Bravo* was the exposure of the crew of the Japanese fishing boat *Lucky Dragon #5 (Daigo Fukuryū Maru)* that occurred at 6:45 a.m. on March 1, 1954. The fishing boat was far out into the Pacific Ocean, northeast of the established international exclusion zone surrounding the Enewetak and Bikini nuclear test sites. Oishi Matashichi, one of the *Lucky Dragon* crew, describes, "a yellow flash [that] poured through the porthole." Scrambling on deck, he saw the "[ship's] bridge, sky, and sea burst into view, painted in flaming sunset colors." Over the next few minutes, the spot on the horizon changed to reddish-purple before "the calm sea went dark again."[30]

Initially confused as to what had happened, the crew started to pull in their fishing lines when a low rumbling sound engulfed them, reminding one of them of "*pika-don*," literally the "flash-boom" experience Hiroshima and Nagasaki atomic bomb survivors remembered. It became clear to the crew that it was "*pika-don*"[31] when daylight illuminated the enormous rising mushroom cloud that slowly covered the sky above them.

After about two hours, it began to rain droplets containing small, white, ash-like particles. Then only the white ash fell. "It was like sleet. As it accumulated on deck, our feet left footprints." In his book years

---

[30]   Oishi, *The Day The Sun Rose In The West*, University of Hawai'i Press, Honolulu, 2011, p. 18-21.

[31]   Ibid, p. 20.

later, after realizing what had occurred, Oishi wrote, "The silent white stuff that stole up on us as we worked was the devil incarnate, born of science. The white particles penetrated mercilessly—eyes, nose, ears, mouth; it turned the heads of those wearing headbands white. We had no sense that it was dangerous. It wasn't hot, it had no odor. I took a lick; it was gritty but had no taste."[32] For six more hours, they worked pulling in their fishing lines. Finished, they headed back to Yaizu, and made port on March 14.

Radiation sickness symptoms in the *Lucky* Dragon crew first appeared the night of exposure, with bouts of pain, headache, nausea, dizziness, and diarrhea. Blisters began appearing, especially around areas where the white ash had accumulated under their clothing. Bunches of hair began falling out a week after exposure. Upon arrival home, a long, painful treatment for radiation sickness began, with hospitalization that lasted until May 1955. Feeling better but not cured, they fearfully awaited the long-term effects of radiation damage to their internal organs.

Meantime, the Japanese people were becoming frightened of the high radioactivity readings in the fish caught in the ocean to the east, and the radioactivity readings in rain and snow that had been increasing over most of Japan. The U.S. initially ignored Japanese complaints and requests for compensation. Finally, in January 1955, Japan was paid $2,000,000 in reparation to the crew of the *Lucky Dragon*. It took the "radiation-related" death of one of the radioman, Kuboyama, in September 1954, to get the U.S. to react. Koboyama died from hepatitis caused from the many blood transfusions required to treat the estimated 330 rad dose he had received. The U.S. also increased the exclusion zone around the Pacific Proving Grounds eight-fold. Over the years, the slow progressive damage from high doses of radiation showed up in all the crewmembers in the form of various cancers and hepatic cirrhoses.[33]

The events surrounding the *Lucky Dragon* and the people of Japan, as they unfolded over the years following Castle Bravo, may have been

---

[32]   Ibid, p. 20.
[33]   Ibid, p. 81.

relatively minor in comparison to the impact on the people living on Rongerik, Rongelap, and Alinginae Atolls. These unfortunate people were accidentally exposed to the fallout and initially ignored, then used as guinea pigs for radiation effects studies by the U.S. I do not intend to describe the ensuing events and problems for the exposed Micronesians that followed, since I was not aware of their exposure at the time. I had heard about the *Lucky Dragon* and only wondered if another mistake might happen during *Oak*. (Interested readers are encouraged to read the recent book by Barbara Johnston[34] to add detail to this horrifying incident.)

What happened during Castle *Bravo* that allowed the *Lucky Dragon* to become engulfed in deadly fallout? It may have been a combination of mistakes made by the fishing boat crew, the Castle Bravo test planners, and the physicists who designed the nuclear device.

The crew of the *Lucky Dragon* appears to have been ignorant of how close they were to the boundaries of the U.S. nuclear test exclusion zone. If they knew they were close, prudent behavior should have warned them to standoff for safety. Hiroshima and Nagasaki had been obliterated less than ten years ago. If they did not know about the exclusion zone or their ship's exact position, their exposure might have been an unfortunate result of ignorance.

Weather prediction is an inexact science even now, and it was not nearly as reliable in 1954. Nevertheless, was there enough uncertainty in the forecast for March 1 to postpone the test? The U.S. could have asked for a larger exclusion zone to cover unusual weather conditions that could lead to radioactive fallout in international areas, or they could have conducted extensive patrols on the extant exclusion zone during larger yield tests. After *Oak,* the Navy significantly expanded the exclusion zone. It is clear that the exposure of the fishermen on the *Lucky Dragon* and inhabited atolls to the east of Bikini Atoll was due to an unfortunate combination of mistakes made by several parties. However, a design error in the LASL device amplified the impact of all

---

34   Johnston, Barbara R., *The Consequential Damages of Nuclear War: The Rongelap Report*, Left Coast Press, July 34, 2008.

the other errors by allowing massive amounts of radioactive material to
rise into the upper-level winds.

Lucky Dragon appears to have been positioned just outside the
northeastern corner of the exclusion zone when Castle Bravo detonated.
Although outside the exclusion zone, the wind was predicted to blow the
fallout from the 4–6 MT detonation in their direction. As a precaution,
Navy ships monitoring the test were positioned almost due east of Bikini
near the inhabited atolls to report any unexpected radioactive fallout.
The debris from the detonation was predicted to fall into the sea before
reaching the exclusion boundary and lie north and far to the west of
the inhabited atolls.

The actual wind direction was 10–15 degrees to the north of its
predicted path.[35] Although there was concern about possible upper-
atmosphere wind direction changes, a last-minute decision resulted
in continuing the test. The changing upper-altitude wind direction
meant that any radioactive material reaching those altitudes could
travel further to the south than predicted and cause some low-level
radioactivity to fall over inhabited areas. The position of the *Lucky
Dragon* was unknown to the Castle Bravo test officials.

Operation Castle focused on testing various fusion devices capable of
greatly magnifying the yields previously achieved through a pure-fission
(splitting) reaction. The first Operation Ivy test, Mike (November
1952), demonstrated that the fission process could initiate a fusion
reaction by combining isotopes of hydrogen (deuterium and tritium)
in a much more energetic reaction. The Mike device contained liquid
deuterium, which had to start at near absolute zero before the initiating
fission radiation increased its temperature to that of the interior of the
sun. The device, with all its test monitoring and cooling equipment,
was the size of a small multistory building.[36]

The goal of Operation Castle was to test new device designs created
by the physicists and engineers at the LASL and the University of
California Radiation Laboratory (UCRL). In the Castle Bravo device

---

[35]   http://nuclearweaponarchive.org/USA/Tests/Castle.html.
[36]   Rhodes, R. (1995), figures 68-72.

called Shrimp, dry lithium isotopes replaced the liquid deuterium, potentially allowing a much smaller and lighter operational weapon design for the military. Based on laboratory neutron interaction measurements, the room-temperature Shrimp was designed by LASL physicists to have a yield between 4–6 MT. Unbeknownst to the physicists, the lithium(7) isotope contained in Shrimp produced two, not one, neutrons when hit by a fast neutron, and the chain reaction ran away to produce an unexpectedly high yield.

Castle Bravo's yield was 15 MT, nearly three times that predicted. Detonation *Romeo,* later in March 1954, also ran away to about three times the initial predicted yield. Three out of the remaining five Operation Castle devices also exceeded yield predictions. The fusion yields also exceeded expectations, and the hydrogen devices were on their way to becoming operational.

Recalling some of the mistakes made during Operation Redwing that resulted in NRDL personnel being exposed to radioactive fallout on Parry Island, what mistakes were about to happen again during *Oak*?

The Face of Armageddon

Inside the Oak fireball. About a millionth of a second after detonation, the *Oak* fission/fusion process was over. The nuclear material had blown itself apart so much that a chain reaction was no longer sustainable. All the materials in the device, surrounding barge, water, and air, out to a radius of several feet, had been vaporized and raised to a temperature of tens of millions of degrees, with a pressure of over a million atmospheres. The X-rays and neutrons raced outward, leaving the heavier particles behind, creating a radiation front that was further absorbed by the surrounding air as it expanded. The radiation, absorption, re-radiation, and expansion processes continued, cooling the mass to 500,000 degrees Fahrenheit within milliseconds. Then the pressure-driven material expansion caught up with the slowing luminescent front and passed into the undisturbed air beyond, condensing the atmospheric water and causing the inner region to become invisible to the outside world.

Finally, the outer high-pressure shock region cooled and lost its opacity as it raced away toward our island perch, and more quickly than we could follow, the hotter inner luminescent thermal region (fireball) again appeared. This point in the process is called "breakaway," and for *Oak,* it occurred about three seconds after detonation, when the fireball radius was already nearly 5,500 feet. The invisible short-wavelength radiation subsided as the mass continued to expand and cool. By now, the fireball was rising, engulfing atmosphere and sweeping up coral and lagoon water into an enormous column. The ball of fire I was feeling the heat from eventually reached a radius of 1.65 miles.

Thermal pulse. I tried to relax as the heat increased. Time seemed to have stopped. My mind momentarily jumped back to the flight from San Francisco to Kwajalein and then Enewetak. I thought of how I had met Tom while boarding the MATS flight, then back further to Berkeley. To a man, my professors at Cal had extolled the exceptional experiences I would gain from such an adventure. How right they were! Did they even know!

The heat was becoming unbearable and bare spots at my ankles were starting to hurt. The aluminum foil hood I had fashioned for protection was beginning to fail and I thought that the hair on the back of my head might catch on fire. My cotton shirt was too hot to lay against my skin, so I arched my shoulders back and let it hang free against the growing inferno 20 miles away.

Beginning to panic, I recall saying out loud, "I had better turn before my clothing flashes."

The light exceeded the level I thought was safe, and I worried that my high-density goggles could not offer adequate protection. I wanted to peek at the fireball and thought of calling what I was experiencing Armageddon. I knew that "Armageddon" was from the Bible as possibly the site on Mt. Megadon (or Megiddon) of a fortress near Jerusalem, where the final battle between good and evil would take place. I had often thought of Armageddon as a being of indeterminable power and horror. Come to find out, nuclear warfare is often referred to in popular publications as an Armageddon for the human race.[37]

I decided to keep looking away.

Keeping my eyes closed, I turned until I could see the edge of the fireball. Armageddon seemed brighter than the sun, which had always appeared as a dim disk of light through the goggles when I had experimented with them earlier. As I again turned away from the fireball, I opened my eyes inside the goggles and, to my surprise, saw outlines of the trees and objects nearby. The heat and light increased relentlessly. The trees and buildings continued to fade from sight, leaving only faint outlines of their reality.

Have the trees vaporized? I asked myself, knowing otherwise. *When will it stop?*

Those first seconds after detonation were the brightest, confusing me and making my effort to estimate the yield in vain. I had planned to estimate the yield by counting the seconds that elapsed after the first flash when the heat leveled out. If my count reached ten seconds and the heat was still growing, I would be in trouble.

I waited. The visible light penetrating my goggles increased and the heat on my back grew more and more intense. I kept wondering about the count. From our NRDL studies, I knew that for *Oak's* predicted yield of 7.5 MT (actual 8.9 MT), about 70 percent of the thermal energy would have radiated away from the fireball by about S+14. Another 10–20 seconds or so would be required before I could comfortably remove my mask and goggles and face the remaining fireball and growing mushroom cloud.

I squirmed to distribute the heat from my side to my back, not realizing that the peak had arrived and I was now living through a long plateau of thermal radiation that accompanies a mature fireball. I had no idea how many seconds had gone by. Finally, I could detect the light fading and the buildings began to fill in. I had tensed up and tried to relax when I could feel the heat on my back begin to subside.

---

[37] Lifton, R.J. and R. Falk, *"Indefensible Weapons,"* Basic Books, Inc., 1982, pp. 58 and 85.

I waited until the inside of the goggles darkened and peeked out to see the buildings and trees beginning to color, then turned to watch the show. It must have been 30–40 seconds after detonation before I took off the goggles and watched the angry violet-red and brown cloud that had surrounded the remains of the high-temperature fireball.

I had time to reflect on the thermal radiation I had just received. *Hooray, I survived!* Silently, the others were also stirring and watching the frightful display of Armageddon's power. My clothing was still warm, but there were no scorch marks. It did not flash. I had just been exposed to about 8-10 cal/cm² of thermal energy over the area facing the blast, but over a few seconds—not all at once. The incident energy absorption and conduction processes in the exposed material are mathematically complex. Norm Alvarez and Bob Hammond, in the thermal effects branch, were more knowledgeable than I about the physics involved. Bob had assured me that we would not catch on fire while standing on the beach.

Theoretically, crumpled paper exposed to the *Oak* thermal radiation on the beach could have ignited. Rayon is particularly susceptible, as are light cotton fabrics, if they have a dark color. The atmosphere preferentially absorbs the long invisible infrared wavelengths and allows the visible wavelengths to travel further. If a material is dark in color, it absorbs more of the visible wavelengths than if it is white and will ignite at significantly lower exposure levels.

Somewhere in the national film archives for nuclear detonations (I believe from Operation Crossroads, *Able*), there is a time sequence of two birds startled by the light flying up into the camera field of view. One bird had white feathers and the other one had black feathers. As they flew before the camera, the black-feathered bird began to smolder and lose altitude while the white-feathered bird kept flying, presenting a dramatic example of the value of light-colored clothing when exposed to the thermal radiation from nuclear detonations.

My clothing was light colored and of the heaviest cotton I could find. At a distance of 20 miles, it would have taken a much larger yield than *Oak* to ignite the clothing I was wearing. If ignition had occurred, there would have been a dramatic flash of flame and smoke. Without surrounding material that the flame could use as fuel, it would have immediately gone out once the input radiation dropped to a level that would not sustain it. If I foolishly stood still for such an assault, I would have ended up with a charred front surface. (The need for keeping the heat confined is why close placement of wood in a fireplace is important in starting a fire.) On the beach in front of *Oak*, I chose not to take a chance and rotated away from the fireball.

For humans and animals, there is time to find protection from thermal radiation if the yield is over a megaton. (The shock wave is another concern.) In a sub-megaton detonation, the thermal energy arrives in a much shorter interval than from larger yields. Weapons with yields less than 100 KT can cause severe burns before a person can react. For the 20 KT Hiroshima and Nagasaki detonations, approximately 70 percent of the thermal radiation arrived in less than one second to produce horrible burns on unprotected people.

However, skin protection for *Oak* was a concern. At an exposure level of 10 cal/cm^2, at a range of 20 miles, we might have received a second-degree burn if we'd faced the fireball throughout the full thermal pulse. In retrospect, the aluminum facemasks were probably not a good idea. I do not remember why we chose to use aluminum foil instead of a white, wet towel, which was readily available. I think it was Tom Dahlstrom's idea and I agreed since he worked in the thermal radiation group. Anyway, the masks worked, even though it got hot behind them.

Earthquake and crater. Whereas a deep underground nuclear detonation the size of *Oak* could produce a significant seismic event, a surface burst transfers a much smaller fraction of its energy into the pressure or shear wave that we experience from an earthquake. The fact that *Oak* was in a barge with an intervening water layer allowed even less detonation energy to be transferred into the bottom to produce a shockwave. I remember feeling a sideways motion, but I'm not sure exactly when. A shear wave that provides the swaying motion would have arrived at our beach between 30-40 seconds after detonation, when I was fixated on the rising mushroom cloud. If a compression wave had formed, it would have arrived earlier and been lost to me in my concern about catching on fire.

The fireball vaporized and blasted out a crater in the seafloor 12 feet beneath the barge that was 5,740 foot in diameter and 204 feet deep.[38] In Operation Ivy, *Mike*, (first hydrogen bomb, 1952), Ulugelab Island, northeast of where *Oak* detonated, completely disappeared from the atoll. What remained in place of Ulugelab was a crater 6,240 feet (1.9 km) in diameter and 164 feet (50 m) deep.[39]

Sonic Boom. After removing the goggles, I continued to watch the rising cloud as it started to form the mushroom cap that characterizes a surface nuclear detonation and waited for the *Oak* sonic boom to arrive. After "breakaway," from the fireball, the pressure front traveled faster than the speed of sound and reached three miles from surface zero with a velocity still above Mach 1. At that distance, the peak overpressure was over twice ambient and decayed to normal pressure within 4 seconds. A brief 400 mph wind followed the shock front.

Two potentially destructive processes occur as the pressure front travels through the atmosphere. A leading peak overpressure arrives that rapidly diminishes in magnitude and increases in duration with distance from surface zero. As the overpressure diminishes, it falls below the ambient pressure, creating a rarefaction (partial vacuum) interval before returning to ambient conditions. This dynamic process generates a wind directed away from the burst, then toward it following the pressure reversal. Although the short overpressure causes the most significant damage to humans and many types of structures, the wind, although brief, is longer than the increased pressure and is highly destructive at closer distances to the detonation.

The shock damage precautions for the lightly constructed atoll buildings I described earlier were in place. Light aircraft flew to positions 35 miles southeast of Enewetak Island where they orbited the

---

[38]   http://nuclearweaponarchive.org/USA/Tests/Hardtack1.html.
[39]   https://en.wikipedia.org/wiki/Ivy-Mike.

USS Boxer while the milder shock front passed.[40] We were given strict instructions (which some of us ignored) to sit down and face away from the blast. Official warnings were distributed everywhere so that no one on the island would be surprised by the blast wave.

We had a little over 90 seconds after detonation to prepare for a series of overpressure shocks followed by smaller rarefaction waves and their associated sonic booms. As the shock front moved toward us, I could see a vertical shadow approach in the distance, slightly to my right. I instinctively opened my mouth and moved my jaw side to side, preparing to equalize any pre-existing pressure difference across my eardrums, closed my eyes, and put my hands over my ears.

POW!

It hit me like a full body slap, knocking me back a bit but not off my feet. I opened my eyes to see another shadow approaching from a slightly different direction. Again, *SLAP*, but not as hard as the first boom. I relaxed and over the next few seconds felt several smaller, non-consequential blows created by reflections off different atoll islands. Surface bursts do not generate shock magnitudes as high as airbursts. Military planners consider the level of damage needed to defeat a target when selecting a weapon's detonation altitude. *Oak*, at its optimum altitude for shock damage, would generate a peak pressure almost double that it produced at sea level.

The *Oak* shock event was much weaker than I'd expected. The peak overpressure on the first shock wave was about 0.6 psi and fell rapidly. I do not remember the rarefaction follow-up, and the wind briefly peaked at about 20 mph, just enough to make me sway a bit while keeping my balance. The slap seemed similar to what we get from friends at play. I was disappointed that it did not knock me down.

Mushroom cloud. While the above phenomena were taking place, the *Oak* fireball kept expanding and climbing at over two hundred miles per hour, reaching an altitude of about 2 miles above sea level at

---

[40]   Gladeck, F.P., et. al., Operation Hardtack I-1958, DNA 6038F, 1 Dec. 1982, AD-A136819, p. 207.

S+15–20. As it cooled, the entrapped vapors condensed, forming the characteristic mushroom cloud stem and obscuring the angry, turbulent purple, red, and brown patches of still-hot material. By about S+60, the boiling mass 20 miles away had turned into a mixture of white and grey vapor, reaching over six miles above us, and was still rising, but more slowly. By approximately two minutes following the detonation, the rising cloud had reached the tropopause, which must have been at about 40,000 feet at our latitude, and began to expand laterally to form the mushroom cap.

The boiling mass slowly continued its climb until it reached about 100,000 feet within 10 minutes. I had to tilt my head back to watch. From our perspective 20 miles away, the leading edge of the cap had already reached 20 miles high; it was like looking at the top of a 50-foot tree from only 60 feet away (Fig. 17). The cloud was stabilizing but the cap radius kept expanding until its outer edge was directly above us. I kept watching for several minutes longer as the cap blanked out more and more of the sky above. JTF-7 had told us that the cloud cap might reach over us, but we were assured that the wind would carry any fallout far out to sea before reaching the surface. Although it contained radioactive material that was emitting gamma radiation, it was too far above us to give us a noticeable dose. However, I kept thinking about Castle *Bravo*, where the fallout pattern did not conform to the pattern predicted.

Tsunami. When the *Oak* fireball began to rise, it drew in water and vaporized the support barge and bottom material. The enormous crater dug out of the bottom coral was just part of the material drawn up into the air in the form of a hollow column. The rising fireball sucked water out of the lagoon, causing a slow withdrawal from our shoreline as we watched, some 10 minutes after the mushroom cloud had formed. It was amazing, just like watching a small tsunami effect on a distant shore before a disastrous aftermath. Surely, we all knew that the water would return.

We watched as the water receded like a curtain being pulled back and the bottom slowly appear. My snorkeling playground revealed itself.

A surprising amount of junk appeared along with small coral groupings and, finally, the swimmer raft rested on the bottom. Shortly, the shark netting that protected us lay on the bottom. To my surprise, two or three people from other organizations walked onto the new beach to examine various objects. We all watched, curious but too afraid to follow. Finally, the water stopped receding, and from where I stood, appeared to form a "wall" like the pictorials of Moses parting the sea. The "wall" seemed to remain motionless for an eternity. Finally, the spell broke as the wall began moving back toward us.

The lagoon water was very shallow, so the wall of water may have been only a few yards high and was maybe 100-200 yards out from the original shoreline. It was difficult to tell how high or how far away it was against the background water surface. I knew that it was coming back and would swamp the beach where we stood, but to what extent—one foot or ten? We scrambled further up the beach, climbed up on the 4x4, and waited. The new lagoon bottom explorers ran back away from the returning water.

The water did not come directly toward us, as it appeared when receding, but as a large breaking wave that angled to the beach to my right. I watched as the wave neared the Scripps Institution of Oceanography pier that extended out from the shore to the north. Water and spray engulfed the structure. It kept coming and, joining with our "wall," engulfed our beach, tossing the buoys about and hissing and gurgling up to the wheels of our vehicle. The water then receded for a second time, exposing a smaller part of my snorkeling area. It came repeatedly in smaller and smaller, and finally minuscule, oscillations of the lagoon surface that lasted all day, but none nearly as dramatic as the first wave.

Radioactive Fallout. The radioactive cloud rained down on the sea far away from us to the west of the atoll. B-57 sampling aircraft followed the cloud as its growth stabilized and recorded that the lower portion of the cloud continued to the west. Its upper portion remained in our vicinity for several hours and eventually moved to the southwest from Enewetak Atoll. Water sampling in the lagoon and on the islands showed no radioactivity except near Bokoluo, where the average radiation level was 0.035 R/hr. Later reports of the extent of the fallout showed that a hot line of radioactivity extended southwest 200 nautical miles 24 hours after detonation, with readings about 0.040 R/hr.[41]

Post-*Oak* Reflections

I walked back to the compound with some of the others. We didn't know it at the time, but *Oak* had exceeded the predicted 7.5 MT and produced 8.9 MT of explosive energy, which generated the heating we experienced under our clothing and aluminum shields. At a distance of 20 miles, the increased yield did not make a noticeable difference in the magnitude of the physical assault that we anticipated. We had escaped the prospect of another Castle *Bravo* misfortune.

We talked about what we had seen, and some compared *Oak* with *Walnut*, which had taken place across the atoll after *Umbrella*. *Walnut* had had a yield of 1.5 MT and had also been a barge detonation but was considerably less spectacular. *Poplar*, scheduled later at Bikini Atoll, was to have a yield of 9.3 MT and was the only detonation larger than *Oak* in Operation Hardtack I. Overall, there were six detonations at Enewetak and Bikini Atolls and two at Johnson Island with yields in the megaton range during Operation Hardtack I.

I remember that we reflected on just how large a yield the weapons could conceptually have. Apparently, a 10 MT device was operational! Could there be a 100 MT device? My world was, thank heaven, confined to the ASROC-size weapons needed by the Navy. However, we speculated about larger yields, and I made estimates of how large a 100 MT bubble would be for a deep-depth/deep-water underwater burst like *Swordfish*. My slide rule gave a bubble maximum radius of just over one mile! Ridiculous—what good would that be? The shock pressure also scales with the cubic root of yield, so it is not optimum to just keep making underwater weapon yields larger and larger. I quit thinking about such things and went back to work.

---

[41]   Ibid, p.207.

It was years later that I learned that *Oak* was the fifth largest nuclear weapon to be tested by the U.S. Our strategic single weapon yields were less than 10 MT. The largest in our inventory, the untested original B-41, was theoretically 25 MT and designed to be bomber-delivered.[42] It was rescaled as a smaller ICBM warhead and finally retired in 1976. Multiple independently targetable reentry vehicles, which attain sufficient destructive power over a wider area, were more effective in destroying hard targets. The Soviet Union tested weapon designs of much greater yield for possible use against cities. They tested several devices with yields between 10 and 25 MT in the early 1960s. These tests gave urgency to the U.S. proceeding with Operation Dominic (1962) in order to verify our warhead designs before signing the Partial Nuclear Test Ban Treaty the following year.

On October 31, 1961, the Soviet Union tested Tsar Bomba in their test range in the Novaya Zemlya archipelago.[43] The name Tsar Bomba appears to be a nickname for a particular Soviet nuclear weapon and often related to the Russian idiomatic expression "Kuzma's mother, or Kuzka's mother." It can mean "to teach someone a lesson, (or) to punish someone in a brutal way." The name appeared about the time of Nikita Khrushchev's shoe-banging incident at a United Nations meeting and his phrase "We will bury you." There are many descriptions on the web of the Soviet Tsar Bomba device and its test that provide images of the fireball and mushroom cloud, as well as abundant references describing the effects observed at great distance.

The weapon's original design had a yield of 100 MT. Because of the enormous amount of fallout predicted and safety concerns for the Tu-95V delivery aircraft, the yield was reduced to about 50 MT. Tsar Bomba was dropped by parachute from an altitude of 6.5 miles and detonated at an altitude of 2.5 miles. This allowed the aircraft to reach safety at a distance of 28 miles before the shock wave arrived. Twenty-eight miles!

42   https://en.wikipedia.org/wiki/B41_nuclear_bomb.
43   https://en.wikipedia.org/wiki/Tsar_Bomba.

In comparison with *Oak*, which had a smaller yield by a factor of five and detonated at the surface, we would have perished at our location on Sonoma Beach. I used NUKEMAP[44], a nuclear weapons effects model based on the work of Carl F. Miller, who was an NRDL employee at the time the laboratory closed to estimate the results of a Tsar Bomba detonation on the surface (as with *Oak*) in San Francisco, California:

Fatalities: 1,251,770 + 999,560 injuries
Fireball radius: 3.8 mi.
Radiation radius: 3.1 mi. @ 500 rem (prompt radiation, full exposure during event)
Air blast radius:
Complete destruction 1.8 mi. @ 20 psi
Most structures destroyed 10.0 mi. @ 5 psi,
Windows broken 27 mi. @ 1 psi
3rd degree burns: 32 mi. @13 cal/cm^2 (full duration exposure on skin)
Maximum dose rate downwind cloud fallout distance/width contours (see NUKEMAP for estimates of total dose): 100 rads per hour: 516/102 mi.

As an air burst, the thermal and shock overpressure from Tsar Bomba would have been greater than the above estimates, however there would be far less sever fallout due to the high detonation altitude and less fireball interaction with the ground. The Soviet detonation caused the complete destruction of the village of Severny, located 34 miles from ground zero. The mushroom-cloud stem was 25 miles wide, and the cap reached 200,000 feet.

Although I will never forget what I saw and felt at *Oak*, Tsar Bomba was designed to be an inhumane city-buster and unimaginably more destructive than my Armageddon. Fortunately, it appears to be too large to effectively deploy in the near future and lower yield options are

---

[44]   NUKEMAP by Alex Wellerstein, https://nuclearsecrecy.com/nukemap/

preferred. The above nightmare of Tsar Bombe luckily can most likely be disregarded in current war planning.

What were U.S. and Soviet Union politicians, military planners, and scientists thinking? Had they actually witnessed one of these weapons in person at close range as I had? Have they even read descriptions of the human suffering and devastation created in Hiroshima and Nagasaki? How many of our military and political leaders today have an Armageddon experience to help guide their decisions?

CHAPTER 9

Interim Report

I left Parry Island on July 2, 1958, for home, having experienced just 45 days in that extraordinary environment: nuclear Armageddon in the midst of tropical beauty. Many of my colleagues in the engineering support groups began leaving for home as soon as they completed their responsibilities after *Umbrella*. They had arrived before *Wahoo*, much earlier than I, and needed to get home. Glynn Pence, part of the field engineering team responsible for setting up our facilities and unpacking coracles and other equipment, arrived on March 30. He remained until just after *Oak* and might have been one of the longest-serving members of our team on Parry. Glynn probably also lost the most weight among our group (205 down to 185 pounds) due to the physical work he performed daily in that climate.

Evan, Tak, and Lou also arrived early with the Project 2.3 support personnel and wanted to see their families as soon as they could. However, JTF-7 required them to remain on Parry until they produced an interim report. All NRDL project leaders remained sequestered until they produced a written summary of their project's activities in *Wahoo* and *Umbrella* and characterized the collected data. As data analysts, Walt and I left as soon as we gave Evan the material he needed to satisfy JTL-7. We were looking forward to spending time together on Waikiki Beach.

Time to Myself

The days between *Umbrella* and *Oak* were idyllic. Finished with *Umbrella* preparation and data collection, I had time to undertake the leisure activities I described earlier. Work hours were regular except when anomalies appeared in the data that required nighttime hours to resolve. Lucky me: up early for breakfast, a swim, off to the compound for work, break for Lou's gym workout, a swim, lunch, back to the compound, knock off for a swim before cocktails in the barracks or at the SBC, dinner, a movie and mischief, and off to bed. Sundays were even more relaxed and gave me time to explore the beaches and study for my impending, or so I thought, exams.

I spent much of my free time during this period alone snorkeling, wandering along the outside reef, or just sitting on the beach. I guess I needed the time alone to think about what was going on around me and what it all meant. I had a fascinating job on a "South" Pacific island (Enewetak is north of the equator, but I always think of having been on an island in the South Pacific). I was witnessing what might be the last large, open-atmosphere thermonuclear weapons tests. I hoped that the multi-megaton tests drawing us closer to nuclear war would no longer be required. (Eight open-atmosphere thermonuclear detonations greater than 1 MT took place in 1962 during Operation Dominic.)

I had a nagging feeling that we were creating something evil. It didn't ruin the pleasure I experienced from living in paradise, but it took something away from the beauty around me. From discussions with my colleagues, I was becoming aware of some scientists' concern that radioactive fallout thrown high into the atmosphere and distributed around the world was causing a long-term hazard to innocent people. These thoughts occasionally appeared then thinking about the school and fraternity activities I would enjoy upon returning home. Did defense scientists concern themselves about such matters?

Radioactive fallout from nuclear testing, by both the U.S. and Soviet Union, had become an international issue by late 1954, after Castle *Bravo*. At NRDL, I learned that scientists detected radioactive fallout from nuclear tests in Nevada in the atmosphere across the U.S.

Radioactive traces of nuclear tests also showed up 30,000 feet above Paris, France.[45] Was this too high a price to pay to have nuclear weapons in our arsenal? I did not think so because of my growing concern for nuclear defense—but still. It was all very confusing.

In 1958, although aware that worldwide fallout from nuclear testing was happening, I did not know much about its potential for causing an increase in various cancers due to radionuclide ingestion and inhalation. Few people had suffered exposure to an external high radiation field at that time. However, we had occasionally discussed the subject back at NRDL, and our entire biomedical sciences division was working on the problem. So there was obviously a danger to humankind—but how much danger? I sensed that we skirted around the problem while conducting our defense research. How could we minimize the radioactive fallout problem using the knowledge we were gathering? However, the Soviets were rapidly developing nuclear weapons to destroy us. Worse, could we live through a Soviet nuclear attack? San Francisco was probably on their target list. Could I escape? I had too many questions to think about while sitting under a palm tree watching the surf. I could think more about it when I returned home.

The Interim Report

The interim report was required to contain information about *Wahoo* and *Umbrella* preparations and data-collection procedures, as well as selected initial results from both tests. Since *Wahoo* took place on May 17, there was time to process some of its data, even while preparing for *Umbrella*. Most of the work for the interim report focused on the data from *Umbrella*.

Evan guided the data analysis, report preparation, and writing tasks as though he were conducting a symphony orchestra. He was involved in and making decisions about every aspect of the work. Tak assisted him by assembling technical material, and Lou provided logistic and

---

[45]   Miller, Richard, *Under the Cloud, The Decades of Nuclear Testing*, The Free Press, A Division of Macmillan, Inc., New York, 1986, p. 162.

communications support with the JTF-7. The JTF-7 audience was waiting to know if we had succeeded in meeting our field objectives and had gathered sufficient information to justify the project's cost. In addition to Project 2.3, there were other NRDL project groups associated with our underwater tests who were also writing interim reports.[46] I worked on whatever material Evan gave me but found my time centered on reconstructing the movement of the free-floating FPs (Fig. 18) and organizing the data related to the physical development of the base surge and radiation fields that would later be associated with the GITR records.

It took nearly two years to turn JTF-7's interim report to a final report, and another year to reach publication.[47] The original interim test report and Project 2.3 final reports were classified "Secret Restricted Data" and contained "critical military information that could reveal system or equipment vulnerabilities," as identified by the Atomic Energy Act of 1954. In their entirety, these reports are still classified. I believe that I have faithfully maintained the line between what is still restricted classified information and the extracted information in what follows, as well as in the earlier parts of this memoir.

Evan and Tak's unclassified final report is truly a memory crutch, since neither I, nor any of my colleagues, can recall the details of our day-to-day data analysis work while on Parry. Much of the information in the extracted version, describing scheduled activities, instrumentation, deployment plans, and theoretical aspects of the phenomena I witnessed, was classified at the time and are available today only because of the government funded Nuclear Test Review Program.[48]

In the early 1980s, a number of ex-NRDLers and I participated in a massive DOD study of civil lawsuits citing health problems related to exposures received during participation in nuclear weapon tests.

---

[46]   Report responsibility fell upon the NRDL project managers: Projects 2.1 and 2.2, Michael Bigger; Project 2.8, Richard Soule (cloud sampling using rockets); Project 3.8; Project 8.4, Al Covey, and Projects 5.1, 5.2, and 5.3, Norman Alvarez (thermal measurements from aircraft).

[47]   Evans, and Shirasawa, 1985.

[48]   http://www.dtra.mil/SpecialFocus/NTRP/NTRPHome.aspx.

The DOD had come under pressure to answer the growing number of lawsuits regarding participant cancer claims. The program provided the public with previously classified and sensitive data from reports issued between 1945 and 1962 that described the weapons tests and associated research. The objective was to "facilitate studies of the low levels of radiation received by some individual participants." As I recall from Hardtack I data, there were very few situations were a participant received enough radiation to have to leave the test site. In addition, to my knowledge no serious radiation exposures occurred.

A summary of *Wahoo and Umbrella* physical and radiological events is provided here to complement the theoretical descriptions of underwater nuclear bubbles and their surface events given in Chapter 7, and to give an overview of the magnitude and nature of the radiological phenomena associated with tactical underwater nuclear weapons. Details of the data collection and analysis efforts are provided for interested readers in the Appendix.

Column and Base Surge Dynamics

There are two columns and base surges associated with an underwater nuclear detonation: one, the visible envelope of water vapor, and two, the inner radionuclide mass that creates the radiological hazard we were investigating. Time photography provided a record of the visible column and base surge development, while GITR records traced the rise and fall of the invisible gamma free-field contained inside. Correlated, the two separate records gave a description of the complex sequence of interrelated events.

A considerable amount of information from Evan and Tak's final report remains classified, leaving only a general description of the physical and radiological above-surface events for summary here.

The *Wahoo* bubble passed through its first maximum radius and broached the surface just prior to contracting to its first minimum (see Chapter 7). The *Umbrella* bubble vented the surface well before it reached its first maximum radius. The resulting difference in internal bubble pressure when broaching the surface might explain some of the differences in the column and base surge dynamics we observed. The maximum column diameter for *Wahoo* was 2,000 feet, with a corresponding height of 1,500 feet. *Umbrella's* maximum column diameter and height were 1,900 feet and 5,000 feet, respectively. In addition, there was speculation from some observers that *Umbrella* had a hollow core, while *Wahoo's* core contained more water vapor.

As the column fell and created the base surge, the expanding water vapor and radionuclide surge front for both events exceeded 40–60 knots during the first minute. The *Wahoo* front initially moved considerably faster, but also slowed more rapidly than *Umbrella's* surge front. By four to five minutes after detonation, both expansions had come to rest, and the base surge moved as a whole only by the wind, which averaged about 15 knots. The visible crosswind radius of both base surges was roughly 7,000 feet when the radial expansion ceased.

Separating the internal radiological surge from the visible water vapor was difficult; only a rough agreement between them was possible from the data we poured over back at NRDL. The two events seemed to move with the same dynamics but were not the same body of material. In general, the base surge developed into a roughly circular torus with defined internal and external lobes of different density material. Spatial irregularities taking place during bubble collapse appear to have a significant influence on the dose a ship receives. *Wahoo's* falling column appeared to produce two expanding toroids with more complex internal structure than did *Umbrella's* column. The data suggested that the radiological cloud inside the *Wahoo* base surge trailed behind the visible leading edge by about 1,000 feet. The radiation was likely associated with the inner torus. In contrast, *Umbrella's* radiological cloud seemed to be associated with the leading edge of the visible base surge.

Base Surge Radiation Field

Naval commanders at sea might not have been interested in all the technical details we were unraveling in the Hardtack I data. They would be interested in the operational protocols developed from what we learned. Ship commanders want to know what to do in order to minimize the radiation harm to his sailors and how to best continue their mission if they become engulfed in radioactive base surge. The ship might be required to operate in and or near the visible base surge to pick up personnel in the water, continue prosecution of an enemy submarine, or for any of a number of other reasons.

GITRs and FPs provided significant data relating to these tactical questions. Project 2.3 arrays of coracles and FPs provided the information needed to generate isodose contours around surface zero. Project 2.1 (another NRDL project at Hardtack I) GITRs and FPs aboard the array target ships extended the measurements onboard and into the ship's interior. From these contours, and the shipboard GITRs, NRDL models could derive the ship radiological risk at any location, or during a transit through, or away from, the detonation.

Data analysis confirmed our predictions and provided details regarding the major sources of radiation risk to ships in a nuclear exchange at sea. The base surge gamma free-field constitutes the major hazard. The contribution to the total dose at any position in the array from column radiation, and radiation from the fallout deposited in the water or ship deck, was minor in comparison to that from the airborne enveloping base surge. Any residual radioisotopes and radiation on the ship's deck produce a long-term radiological hazard and need removing as soon as possible.

A major complicating factor in predicting the shipboard dose is the self-shielding from metal structures, which vary at different locations aboard the ship. An estimate of the unobstructed solid-angle exposure to the base surge at each instrument position aboard the ships compared well with the total dose received during both events. All the ships except one had a full washdown system in operation until well after the base surge subsided. On these ships, radioactive nuclides continuously wash off the deck and vertical surfaces into the surrounding sea.

Shipboard washdown systems at Hardtack I consisted of a series of pipes and nozzles spread over decks and superstructures to generate a "car-wash-like" shower for the entire ship. Early after Operation

Crossroads, the Navy realized that such systems could significantly reduce the amount of contaminated material sticking to ship surfaces and reduce the problems it produces. (Recall Crossroads' contamination problems leading to the establishment of NRDL. Removing these radioactive nuclides is not easy.) Operation Castle (1954) was the first test of washdown system efficacy. On modern warships, pressurization of the manned internal spaces eliminates internal contamination from nuclear, biological, and chemical attacks. Most of the GITR and FP dose came from the base surge gamma free-field, although dose rate rapidly increases when entering a drifting patch of foam or white water containing radioactive bottom material.

Dose rates in both events peaked between 10,000 and 100,000 R/hr for many of the close-in coracles and ships during the first minute after detonation. (10,000 for one or two minutes could produce a dangerous radiation dose.) All records showed a characteristic increase in the dose rate as the radioactive cloud within the base surge approached, then leveled off and decreased as the torus passed. Unfortunately, interior surge lobes, overturned coracles, and ship motion constantly varied instrument shielding and exposure to the radiation field. Considerable spiking in the data records made it difficult to assess the contribution of specific base surge components.

Ship deck doses, accumulating over the entire radiological event, showed that *Wahoo*'s was almost a factor of two higher at a similar distance from surface zero. For example, the average dose along the deck of the DD 592, located about 3,000 feet downwind, was 500 rad for *Wahoo* and only 300 rad for *Umbrella* (both serious levels of radiation). A similar trend followed for other distances from surface zero. Close-in *Wahoo* stations received a much higher total dose than *Umbrella* stations, while the more distant stations received less. Figure 19 shows the *Umbrella* base surge expansion at various times and an estimated total dose received at each of the ship positions.

Details of the radiation exposure levels are missing from Project 2.3's extracted report and are not available for public release. The above general description of these events, which I gleaned from the report, provides only a sense of the magnitude of their radiological characteristics. Whereas differences between the two underwater detonations can be compared to help build an understanding of the radiological hazards associated with Navy tactical nuclear weapons, there is little comparison to above-water detonations. Effects from Shot *Oak* (Chapter 8), a strategic weapon, and Shot *Umbrella*, an underwater tactical weapon, cannot be compared. *Umbrella* did not have *Oak's* accompanying thermal and shock phenomena and was 1,000 times smaller in yield. They are essentially incomparable events.

What If?

I recall that I began thinking about the difference in destructive effects between *Umbrella* and *Oak* immediately after witnessing Armageddon. We all worried, not about the base surge and phenomena we experienced in *Umbrella*, but what would happen if a strategic warhead, a Soviet *Oak*, detonated over the San Francisco area where we worked. (Today, *Umbrella*-size nuclear detonations are more on the public's mind, since lower-yield nuclear weapons appear to be more readily available to terrorists and countries experimenting pursuing a nuclear deterrent. Acquiring and delivering a thermonuclear weapon the size of *Oak* is possible but much more unlikely.) While working on the interim report, I also worried about what would happen if either an *Umbrella* or an *Oak* were to detonate in the San Francisco Bay Area? A Tsar Bomba event was beyond reality for me in those days.

Figure 20 is a map of San Francisco and surrounding area to about 20 miles. If an *Umbrella*-like device detonates off a ship near one of the piers (for example, AT&T Park today), the resulting base surge, at about 5 minutes, would extend out to the dark circle shown. Afterward, the falling column energy depleted, the base surge would continue to travel with the prevailing wind—most likely toward Oakland. Unless the wind were higher than a few knots, it is unlikely that significant radiological dose from the fallout would reach Oakland because particulate deposition and mixing in the bay water would rapidly deplete the airborne radioactive cloud.

A significant exposure to radiation would take place in the San Francisco waterfront area near the stadium, and people breathing the falling mist would have long-range effects from internal absorption of radionuclides. Physical damage would be small relative to an air detonation, which can create the strong, sharp shock wave and thermal effects I described earlier. Although terrible, a small tactical weapon detonated underwater appears to be a wasted effort. A more likely surface or airburst of this size would create much greater havoc on people and buildings.

Thermonuclear weapons, with a thousand times greater yield, also would not produce optimal damage to a civilian environment if detonated underwater because of the shielding produced by even a relatively thin sheath of water around the detonation. Many classified nuclear weapons reports classified during the Cold War give altitudes for creating the maximum thermal or shock effects against civilian populations are now available to the public.[49]

Figure 20 also gives a sense of the difference between *Umbrella* and *Oak*-like events. The *Oak* fireball was over 1 mile in diameter. The shock wave produced at a distance of 3 miles could be 30-40 psi and over 400 mph (estimates I made later at NRDL using the 1962 Nuclear Bomb Effects Computer described in the beginning of Chapter 8). Second to third-degree burns could occur at a distance of over 15 miles to skin exposed for 20-30 seconds, and flammable material could cause flammable material to ignite, spreading the damage caused from the shock wave.

We lived under a general, low-level, but ever-present fear at NRDL during the Cold War period. We understood the Armageddon we might possibly face. Besides the usual fire drills at the lab, we felt that there would be some kind of warning for us through government communication channels. For example, NRDL might receive early warnings of increased Defense Condition Readiness (DEFCON) level, the Joint Chiefs of Staff estimate of the likelihood of war. I don't remember the escape drill, but it wouldn't have made much difference,

---

[49]   Glasstone, et al., 1962.

since we assumed San Francisco was targeted with more than one multi-MT warhead.

While working at NRDL, I often thought about how to escape a possible Bay Area Armageddon. While writing this section of the memoir, I examined some old records of the planning I had done upon returning from Enewetak. I had hoped that any extra warning government workers at NRDL might have would allow a head start on the traffic jam that would follow the civil defense sirens. My additional advantage might have been that I knew which direction to go to flee the Bay Area to safety. I will say more about this escape plan in Chapter 10.

Going Home

As my time on Parry grew short, I began to think about home and the stopover in Hawaii I had planned. I wanted more of the lush, dense foliage and long rolling waves on Waikiki Beach, so different from those I surfed during high school on the strand south of Coronado in San Diego. And I did not want to return to sorority food after enjoying the extravagant buffet tables at the Waikiki Sands Hotel. I was developing a taste for tropical environments that stayed with me the rest of my life.

Before I left Enewetak to return home, I told Evan that I would be stopping in Honolulu for a while. This elicited a story about Dr. Bernard Wheatley, whom Evan had met earlier during a hiking trip on the Kalalau Trail along the Na Pali cliffs, on the northern shore of Kauai Island. Dr. Wheatley, a physician and disenchanted with civilization, had retreated to live as a hermit on Kalalau Beach, 11 miles inland from the trailhead near Hanalei Bay.

Due to its inaccessibility during the late 1950's, Kalalau Beach was nearly deserted. The trail is not just long but also difficult, rising and descending what seems like hundreds of feet as it winds along a narrow path high above the water. Dr. Wheatley had selected a perfect place to retreat to and consider the meaning of his life, and the time he had left. Evan related how he and Wheatley spent a night in a cave discussing the wonders of the world, philosophy, politics, and, I'm sure, the evils of civilization. Evan urged me to "look him up" if I had the opportunity on my way home. He warned me that Dr. Wheatley was shy and would try to avoid human contact. Evan said, "Just shout my name and he will come close to talk."

A hiking trip on Kauai was not part of my plan for the trip home, and it was nearly 10 years later that the chance to meet Dr. Wheatley occurred. It happened during a day-hike I took with my first wife to Hanakapi'ai Valley, the first beach area along the 11-mile Kalalau Trail. The hike to Hanakapi'ai Valley took about two hours, and we arrived at the beach entrance late in the afternoon. The beach was narrow, rocky, and washed by huge waves. A slight cliff overhang lay opposite where we stood, and fearing another shower, we moved toward it to seek shelter. As we approached, I noticed a figure under the overhang close to the wall. Could it be? Was that Dr. Wheatley? I stopped, fearing the figure might retreat into the valley. I called out, "Dr. Wheatley? Evan Evans sends his greetings."

Evan's name worked! The figure moved slowly forward and said, "How is Evan?" I introduced myself while moving slowly forward and we started a hesitant, faltering conversation regarding what Evan was currently doing. Realizing that we were not going to have a lengthy conversation, we soon said our goodbyes, and I promised to pass his regards on to Evan. Dr. Wheatley turned and moved off up the valley. I wondered why he was at the beach end of the valley, so close to civilization. I imagined his dwelling to be further up the river, perhaps near the waterfall about two miles back into the forest. It was getting late and we needed to make the difficult passage to our car before dark.

All the way back to the car, I thought about Evan and his ability to communicate with everyone. It was only many years later after we both had retired did I see him again.

I don't recall leaving Parry, taking the ferry ride to Enewetak, and starting the long journey back to Hickam Air Force Base. Walt has told me we hit Waikiki Beach together on July 4. I had a room at Fort DeRussy, an old shore battery on the island of Oahu designed to provide coastal defense. The guns were silenced in the 1950s, but the Bachelor Officer Quarters was open for business. The location was ideal. A short walk took one to the Hawaiian Village, Kaiser's large hotel complex, or to the main Waikiki Beach spread of hotels. The whole setting was exotic for me, and I spent two or three days at Fort DeRussy and Waikiki Beach lost in their enchantment, but somehow failing to recall many details. Luckily, I had run into Walt Gurney while there and he was able to help me recall an event that he particularly relishes.

We were on the beach outside one of the hotels when we spotted several college girls acting as though they wanted some company. We were both tanned from our membership in the Totally Tan Club on Parry, Walt much more so, and deeper in color than I. But I wore my lava-lava (a colorful native Polynesian sarong extending from the waist to mid-calf), had a rough reddish beard (from laziness) and was therefore appropriately dressed to approach the girls. I did so and managed a little Hawaiian Pidgin English to break the ice. It worked and I struck up a conversation with them, which Walt quickly joined. Smitten by one of the girls, he asked her out that night, continued dating her back in the Bay Area, and ended up marrying her. When recounting this incident to me for the memoir, he said, "You remember Beverly, the tall, good looking one." I can't recall what happened after we left the beach, so I guess I didn't get along all that well with any of the other girls.

The trip back to Travis Air Force Base was uneventful, and I have no memories of the long flight. Wally Anderson met me at the terminal and, as we drove back to Berkeley, I began to realize that I had experienced something both wonderful and horrific.

CHAPTER 10

Mice and Men

I began writing this chapter in my mind again and again before sitting down at my PC to place words on a page. Each time I tried to form the sentences to summarize my short time at Hardtack I, and satisfactorily end my adventure, I realized that there was yet more to tell. My Armageddon experience did not end when I left Parry Island for home. It continued throughout my days at NRDL as my colleagues and I studied the formation and distribution of radiation from nuclear weapons. Most importantly, Parry Island was the beginning of a terrifying understanding of modern warfare. Along the way, I learned more about who I am.

I want to extend my story for a few years after Operation Hardtack I to include recollections from the period that began with Hardtack I but end with the closing of NRDL. Many of my early concerns regarding the value of our work matured by then and influenced my dedication to national defense work, both within and outside government civil service, for over a half a century to come.

This chapter does not parallel Steinbeck's tale about George and Lennie. The title of this chapter came to me shortly after I began to write about the early days of NRDL. The "mice" were the thousands of tiny subjects the NRDL Biological and Medical Science (Biomed) Division scientists sacrificed to study how much exposure "men" can tolerate from gamma, alpha, and neutron radiation. That work, and similar efforts by other national and university laboratories, provided information for developing critical military tactics and medical procedures for dealing with nuclear radiation exposure during a possible hot war with the Soviet Union. (Is it possible this knowledge will again be useful?) Those efforts also helped lead to safety regulations for direct and internal radiation exposure in nuclear power plants, better procedures, in laboratory research and medical treatment using isotopes, and many other civilian innovations and developments.

The Fifth Floor

I infrequently had business on the fifth floor, the home of the biomedical division, or even wanted to visit there because of the odor. In some areas, it was like being in a veterinarian's operating room, and like a doctor's examination room in other sections. The work there involved controlled experiments with small animals and some not so small. The animals lived in breeding colonies and in care facilities designed for the special strains required by the MDs, biochemists, physiologists, and psychologists who occupied the labs.

Although many of the laboratory areas were finished in tile and ventilated to near hospital standards, the lingering mixture of odors throughout the floor unsettled me. Not schooled in biological research methods and medical terminology, such as serum lipoproteins and hematopoietic syndromes, I did not understand the details of the research.[50] My work did not involve the biology of radiation effects, and I was technically lost when visiting the floor. I did know that the

---

[50] Serum lipoproteins are now commonly identified with high- and low-density cholesterol concentrations found in the blood and their relation to heart attacks. Hematopoietic syndrome is a group of clinical features associated with effects of radiation on the blood and lymph tissues characterized by nausea and vomiting, anorexia, lethargy, rupture of blood cells, destruction of the bone marrow, and atrophy of the spleen and lymph nodes.

work was important to what might happen to someone caught in the radiation fields I was studying.

In addition, the fifth floor was a bit spooky, especially late in the evening when nearly everyone had left for home. A humming symphony of blowers circulating air and automated instruments endlessly performing data collection and monitoring tasks overlaid an eerie silence. However, there was a fascination for me about how the results of our radiation exposure efforts might be useful, and occasionally I ventured to the floor below my office.

One night, an incident really disturbed me. Just out of curiosity, I stopped on the fifth floor on the way home. There was always some fascinating laboratory to explore. Stepping out of the elevator, I confronted a tall, slender dog, maybe a greyhound. He stood there looking at me for a moment, then turned and limped away down the hall. It was then that I noticed a wound on his hind leg—with a bone sticking out! I automatically turned and hit the button for the elevator, which had not moved, and tried to decide whether to go after him. Luckily, I heard someone in one of the rooms further down the hall call out to him, allowing me to step into the elevator without guilt. But what kind of research used a dog and created the wound I had seen? Unusual things were happening on the fifth floor.

I later learned that individual experiments included an analysis of bones and tissue of sacrificial animals.[51] (I hoped these experiments were restricted to mice, rats, and monkeys, at worst, and did not include the dog I had seen.) The purpose was to learn how certain long-half-life radioisotopes are concentrated in various tissues after entering the body through inhalation or ingestion. For example, rat livers were kept alive and made to continue functioning entirely outside sacrificed animals that had been exposed to varying amounts of radiation. Rats were tested for their willingness and ability to perform work in a squirrel cage with the hope of learning something meaningful for troops exposed on the battlefield.

---

[51] Hinners, R.A., 1957.

I understood the importance of some of the fifth floor's results. Research showed that laboratory animals exposed in Operation Crossroads were able to survive radiation doses that earlier appeared lethal and that substantial amounts of radioactive material could now be eliminated from the body by prompt treatment. Other research included advances on the effects of ionizing radiation on a test animal's lifespan due to more effective exposure diagnosis, prophylaxis, therapy for radiation injury, and internal radiation-hazard assessment. The impact of the fifth-floor research on understanding radiation impact in military and civilian applications was significant and possibly the most important general product of NRDL's short history.

NRDL's contributions to our nation's defense posture were critically important in that period of the Cold War. Nowhere else in the world was there an establishment where a substantial number of top-level research people in both the physical and biological sciences were working together in a single, closely integrated environment. The words of the first commanding officer, Captain Hinners, summarize this feature of NRDL better than I can:[52]

> In examining the Laboratory's history and present technical position, one aspect in particular stands out. Many of the distinguished scientists and research administrators, both from the U.S. and abroad who have had occasion to visit NRDL have commented that nowhere else in the world do they know of an establishment where a substantial number of top-level research people in both the physical and biological sciences are working together in a single, closely integrated department. This is reflected in the design of the new Laboratory building itself, where the medical and biological scientists are to be found on the fifth floor, the chemists nearby on the sixth and the physicists and electronics scientists on the fourth. It is paying off in ways which go far beyond the obvious advantage to the M.D.'s and biologists of having physicists and chemists close at hand to take over or assist in delicate physical and radio-chemical

---

[52]   Ibid, p. 435.

tests where extreme accuracy is essential for the detection of subtle effects which often seem to be the rule rather than the exception in this field.

Besides trying to understand the research pursued within the walls of NRDL, I was naturally curious about what the impact of an all-out nuclear war with the Soviet Union would be on our society beyond the Bay Area.

Thinking the Unthinkable

Hermann Kahn's book, *On Thermonuclear War*,[53] was heady reading for me when it came out a couple of years after returning from Enewetak. I heard that Mr. Kahn had visited the lab to discuss civil defense with Walmer (Jerry) Strope, then head of the Military Evaluation Division, who later became Assistant Secretary of Defense for Civil Defense. Apparently, Mr. Kahn relied on NRDL research to help formulate his ideas regarding how the U.S. could survive all-out nuclear war with the Soviet Union. My focus was on nuclear war at sea, and I never had a chance to meet, or even see, Mr. Kahn during one of his visits. However, his ideas immersed me in a larger picture of the research we were doing.

In *On Thermonuclear War*, Herman Kahn tackled (as few before him had) the tough issues regarding nuclear war with the Soviets. He had been an analyst for the Rand Corporation since 1948 and delved into the "hard choices" government planners faced when considering the nuclear arms race that was developing. His analysis ranged from examining high-level alternative national postures to the details of survival economics and technology of missile system tradeoffs. A particular chapter title that grabbed my attention was *Will the Survivors Envy the Dead?*—a possibility due to the genetic effects survivors could pass along to future generations. Discussing the possibility of the U.S.

---

[53] Kahn, H., *On Thermonuclear War*, 2nd edition, Princeton University Press, Princeton, New Jersey, 1961.

suffering as many as 160 million deaths from an all-out war with the Soviets, and what our nation should do to survive in the long run, earned him the nickname Dr. Strangelove, from Stanley Kubrick's movie character.

I adopted the title of this section of my memoir from the title of Kahn's later book, *Thinking about the Unthinkable*, which was first published in 1962.[54] Mr. Kahn continued developing the national strategies possible to avoid nuclear war and delved more into the moral issues faced from its potential horrors. But I, among the others at NRDL, lived more with what the details of such a war would have at the personal, human level. I was not so sure that his predictions of how well the U.S. would recover after receiving maybe a thousand times the Hiroshima radiation spread over our military bases and large population centers were valid. I wondered what life would be like after such an attack.

This was before the possibility of a nuclear winter had arisen, which would make human survival even less probable. The effect of hundreds of megaton warheads detonating during a war with the Soviet Union was hypothesized to create a cloud cover over the northern hemisphere that would last years, effectively lowering the earth's temperature so that crop growth would be severely limited and millions of people would perish. (Estimates are that more than 50,000 nuclear warheads were in the final Cold War arsenals.) Most of the impact would be contained in the northern hemisphere where the winds would circulate the atmospheric radioactivity. I had also read *On the Beach*, by Nevil Schute, and seen the movie (1959), which increased my apprehension for those living in the southern hemisphere. To me, the threat of nuclear war with the Soviets was an existential threat to our society. I believe today's nuclear terrorist threat is not an existential concern in the same way. (However, the Cold War doomsday threat of a nuclear exchange with Russia has again risen, and potential conflict between nations with nuclear weapons is of even greater concern today.)

---

[54]   Kahn, H., *Thinking about the Unthinkable*, Horizon Press, New York, 1962.

Why did I think the Soviet threat was so severe? Besides experiencing *Oak* and periodic spooky visits to the fifth floor, I was becoming aware of the concern about surviving a nuclear war taking place at the national level. Dr. Newell, whom I mentioned earlier, Terry Triffit, Paul Tompkins, Ed Alpin, and other NRDL scientists testified before the Congressional Special Subcommittee on Radiation during June 1959, regarding the physical characteristics of fallout, its distribution, and the resulting radiation effects on humans.[55] They were testifying during the time I was analyzing the *Wahoo* and *Umbrella* data at the lab. My colleagues summarized a great deal of information for the subcommittee, which gave me a larger picture of what would occur in the event of all-out nuclear war. The subcommittee report was fascinating reading when it became available after the hearings.

The hearings focused on a scenario describing a successful attack by the Soviet Union against our nation and established what might be a worst-case radiation situation. (The impact on our military effectiveness and physical damage to the U.S. infrastructure was not included in these particular hearings.) The scenarios were concerned mostly with the local and long-range distribution of the radiation across the U.S., as the wind carried fallout far from the initial detonation points. The public needed to be aware of the long-term radiation dangers. Although being concerned with the long-term effects, I was most worried about where to go in order to survive an attack on the Bay Area, where I lived.

Testimony given to the subcommittee by various scientists, economists, and sociologists relied on a hypothetical laydown of nuclear warheads by the Soviet Union on U.S. targets (Fig. 21). The U.S. Office of Civil and Defense Mobilization (OCDM) was not involved in designing the scenario but did make the assessment of effects that would result from 263 warheads delivered to 224 U.S. targets. 192 targets were military installations, and the remaining 71 warheads were projected to impact on industrial installations and population centers.

---

[55] Joint Committee on Atomic Energy, Hearings before the Special Subcommittee on Radiation, *Biological and Environmental Effects of Nuclear War, Part 1*, Washington DC: U.S. Government Printing Office, 1959.

Of the 263 warheads, 60 were 10 MT (*Oak*-size), 74 were 8 MT, and the remaining warheads were between 1 and 3 MT, for a 1,446 MT total yield in the attack. (Later scenarios for an all-out nuclear exchange varied as refinements to the threat were developed. Not strangely, they always seemed to increase the total yield the U.S. would receive in an all-out nuclear attack as predictions of the Soviet capabilities grew. By the time the Cold War ended, the Soviets might have had an order of magnitude more warheads targeting the U.S. than assumed by the subcommittee.)

As horrible as the scenario was, I focused my interested in the San Francisco allotment of Soviet warheads, their number and yields. I decided that the Hunters Point Naval Shipyard was targeted, and that NRDL might be within a fireball, if the estimated Soviet missile aim-point error was achieved. At the time (circa 1960) I had estimated from various sources that the Soviet ICBM Circular Error Probability (CEP) for an 8-10 MT warhead was about 3 nautical miles. CEP is an estimated circular radius in which 50% of the warheads will land. Using Hunters Point Naval Shipyard, or even downtown San Francisco as an aim point, and an *Oak*-like fireball radius of half the CEP, NRDL could be within the fireball in a Soviet attack. Surviving such an attack even if they missed their CEP seemed unlikely.

What would I do? Where would I go? I referred to the OCDM map in Figure 21, which gave the Congressional subcommittee's warhead laydown across the continental U.S. It appeared that due to the concentration of naval installations in the Bay Area (e.g. Hunters Point, Alameda, and Mare Island) as well as being a major population center, San Francisco would draw several high-yield warheads. (The fallout maps provided in the hearings were colored and easier to read.) The U.S. Printing Office reproductions I had available are useful for general information only, since the wind direction controlled the pattern. Escaping beyond the immediate damage zone appeared unlikely without considerable evacuation time following an alert.

I recall that there was some discussion among my NRDL colleagues about an official relocation plan in response to an imminent nuclear attack warning. Paul Zigman, while reviewing my memoir, reminded me that laboratory technical personnel were assigned post-attack safe positions along the coast south of the Bay Area.[56] Sites somewhere south of the Bay Area along the coast were designated holding areas for us upon receipt of a missile launch message, or other emergency alert that an attack was imminent. When asked, none of my colleagues told me how they would have responded to emergency alerts. I do not believe they would have abandoned their families and escaped to the coast. But none remembered, or wanted to talk about, what they would do or even that a safe zone had existed.

What would happen if the U.S. and Soviet situation deteriorated when I was away from the lab? I was concerned, my colleagues were concerned, and the nation was concerned. People were building shelters beneath their homes in hopes of surviving a nuclear war with the Soviet Union. In the U.S., children learned in school how to hide under their desks when the sirens sounded. Does anyone remember how people felt during those times? Neither my kids, nor my grandkids, have any idea what it was like.

I chose to plan for an optimistic situation, in which there would be several hours of warning of a possible attack, or that I became personally scared by a news event. Several years later, the Cuban Missile Crisis gave me an occasion to worry about my evacuation plans. I recall that the threat level status rose to DEFCON 2 on October 26, 1962, and B-52 bombers moved to safer locations. (DEFCON 1 meant imminent war.) Luckily, the weekend was coming up and I did not have to go to work and possibly face a fireball. Things continued to heat up over the weekend but quickly calmed down early the following week. The timing is vague, and I do not recall what I did over the weekend, so perhaps I just kept my fingers crossed.

However, I had a plan for where to go if the bombs were imminent, based on the fallout patterns from the detonations and the prevailing wind. I referred to Figure 22, the OCDM map for the fallout pattern over the U.S. two days (D+2) after an attack. Detonation fallout would continue in the direction dictated by high-altitude winds, as happened

---

56   Personal correspondence with Paul Zigman, December 2016.

with the *Lucky Dragon*. Radioactivity would spread over everything and lodge in the surface soil. After the radioactive clouds passed, the radioactivity in the soil and on surrounding surfaces would continue to increase the dose an unprotected person received.

The situation for the Eastern U.S. would be disastrous because of the prevailing winds. The West Coast was far better off due to fewer warheads being scattered out over a larger area, and the wind direction is predominately east, inland from the coast. I planned to check the weather and go in a direction where the prevailing upper winds did not take the radioactive clouds.

The radiation exposure to an unsheltered public that did not know where to go for safety for a period of weeks or months after the attack could be significant. Inside the patterns shown in Figure 22, (D+2) for example, there are areas where the dose rates are between 0.1 R/hr and could be greater than 30 R/hr. When taking into account arrival time delays, the accumulated dose at D+2 in these areas was projected to be between 75 and 8,000 R.

Fortunately, the dose rate rapidly decreases with time due to radiological decay. However, it was still projected to exceed 0.1 R/hr in about 6% of the country's land mass 3 months later, giving a potential minimum accumulative dose of 200 R. Even more important, these dose estimates do not consider the long-range effects of inhaling the radioactive particles in producing cancer and other health problems, as demonstrated by the *Lucky Dragon* aftermath.

What happens if a radiation shelter is available? During the Cold War, the OCDM provided pamphlets describing designs of fallout and blast protection shelters that families could construct inside or near their homes, if they had nowhere to go to safety.[57] Educating the population about the serious harm they faced if nuclear war broke out became a national goal. A committee of the National Academy of Sciences, in a study of national preparedness, concluded that: "Adequate shielding is the only effective means of preventing radiation casualties."[58] Following

---

[57] *Masonry Family Fallout shelters*, OCDM, MP-18, February, 1960.
[58] *The Family Fallout Shelter*, OCDM, MP-15, 1959.

the OCDM shelter designs provided different levels of protection from the long-term effects from fallout. Direct radiation and blast are more difficult to mitigate, and the public was educated on how to react to an imminent warning of a possible nearby nuclear detonation. The actions recommended did not appear to be particularly effective if the blast was within a couple of miles. Fate seemed to be the only protection one could rely upon.

Besides construction suggestions, the OCDM pamphlets also discussed how to provision the shelter and live in the restricted area of about 10 square feet per person for periods up to 14 days. As the Cold War went on, chemical and biological issues added to the design complexity of protective shelters by increasing inlet air filtering. Although a danger was always present from inhaling airborne radionuclides stirred up by the wind, the early focus was on gamma radiation from fallout material that deposited on the ground around the shelter. Mines, tunnels, and subbasements of multistory buildings could provide a factor of 1,000, or greater, reduction in the exposure received while remaining in a fallout area.[59] Wood-frame houses with the masonry shelter design recommended by OCDM could provide exposure reduction factors between 50 and 250. Exposure reduction between 2 and 10 is possible in the basement and central areas for multistory masonry housing. A typical single-story wood house without a shelter would provide very little protection from radioactive fallout.

Where it was not possible to build underground shelters, the OCDM recommended above-ground shelters. These designs included both 10 and 4-inch thick masonry sidewalls separated by 12 inches of sand and reinforcing metal ties, a 20-inch thick masonry roof, and a blast door capable of withstanding 10 psi overpressure. It was possible to survive a 20 MT airburst at a distance of 5 miles. Other variations in thickness and strength were available for more distant locations where less protection was anticipated.

---

[59]   Paul Zigman related to me the instructions he gave his wife in case he was not at home when the emergency sirens sounded: go directly to Macy's sub-basement in the San Mateo shopping center. December 2016.

Many scientists at NRDL worked on fallout protection at Camp Parks, an old Navy facility east of the Oakland hills in Dublin, CA. They spread radioactive material over the surrounding structures and the ground to simulate the radiation fields associated with fallout. Hard data on the exterior and internal radiation allowed them to evaluate various cleanup and mitigation techniques. Camp Parks was also the site where radiation experiments on larger animals took place and where some of my colleagues conducted underwater experiments with high explosives in preparation for Operation *Wigwam*. A prototype 100-man underground fallout shelter constructed in 1959 for habitability studies was one of the larger structures at Camp Parks. Although I was aware of the work at Camp Parks, I was never part of specific fallout or radiation effects experiments conducted at the facility.

My personal escape option was clear. I would travel either north or south from the Bay Area, as fast as possible. I would NOT go east to Lake Tahoe, for example, to escape the radiation, or east toward the valley to take Highway 99 north or south. I would go directly up or down Highway 101 for about 50 miles. Alternatively, I would head north to Oregon. (The Soviets did not appear to want to bomb the hippies.) I was single in those days and had decided that stealing a motorcycle was the best mode of transportation, if the public was panicked and the roads clogged—all in all, a simple strategy just in case. I still recall feeling confident that I could escape harm given even a short warning about an impending nuclear attack. I told my friends about my plan, but generally, there was a psychological sense of helplessness in the popular thinking of the time.

While writing this section of the memoir, I came upon long-forgotten notes that again reminded me of the concern many had in those days about surviving a nuclear attack. In the early 1960's, I became engaged to my girlfriend, Sue, and began thinking more like my married colleagues. The papers I found contained estimates of kill probability for unprotected people living in a house in an area where Sue's parents lived. I had assumed a single five-megaton weapon detonated on Treasure Island between San Francisco and Oakland, about six miles away.

A yellow and weathered Journal of the American Medical Association article and a Xerox copy of a map of the Bay Area, showing five- and ten-mile radii from Treasure Island, and Sue's parents' house location marked with the number "0.06" are all that remain of the file.[60] I apparently had sifted through the journal article's numerous graphs, and assuming a 5 MT detonation, discovered that the estimated kill probability for an exposed person was 0.94, i.e., the survival probability was 6%.

Estimates of such events are much more sophisticated today, and the journal article is just a curiosity. The authors had used Rand Corporation estimates and Soviet ICBM aiming accuracy estimates (3.5 miles circular probable error) to arrive at lethality estimates from thermal, shock, and nuclear radiation exposures for unprotected, family home basement, as well as purposely designed bomb-shelter environments. Unfortunately, even if the Sue's parents' house had a typical basement to use as a shelter, the survival probability rose to only about 20%.

I cannot imagine how, or even if, Sue and I talked about such matters.

Who Am I?

One of the difficulties faced when writing a memoir so many years after events have taken place is recalling the time and place that specific ideas or thoughts occurred. Physical events are more amenable to placing a time, but the occurrence of an idea or the mental resolution of an issue or problem is more fleeting. What helps fix a particular thought in time is to be able to associate it with a physical event—in this case, an event that caused me to realize something about myself: something that I might have only vaguely thought about before what happened one evening when I was alone in the lab.

---

[60] Russell, Philip W., M.D., and G. Laddie, M.S. Kimbrel, "Estimates of the Kill Probability in Target Area Family Shelters," JAMA, vol. 180, no. 1, April 7, 1962, p. 25-29.

It was mid-evening during the summer of 1963 when I stopped work at my first-floor explosion tank facility in the north end of Building 815 and went home to change clothes for a casual cocktail party at a friend's apartment in the city. The party itself is lost from my mind, and I remember only that I wore my forest-green corduroy suit and that I was driving—somewhere. While working, a dilemma suddenly hit me that caused me to drop what I was doing and accept the party invitation.

I thought, *Should I continue the experiment I had just begun, or immediately stop all further work on it and forget the whole idea?* I suddenly realized that I faced an internal struggle, discovering an inconsistency in my character. The outcome of such dilemmas is seldom as clear as it turned out in this case. After barely an hour at the party, my internal struggle became too much to silently endure making small talk to my friends. I left and returned to the lab to find an answer.

My explosion facility consisted of a large steel tank with an epoxy interior and tall slender glass windows. Inside, I could emulate a small underwater nuclear explosion and study the separation of explosion energy into their different forms: radiant, shockwave, and bubble hydrodynamic energy. The explosion simulated a nuclear underwater detonation, but in the form of electrical energy, discharged in microseconds from a large capacitor bank into a thin wire placed between underwater electrodes.[61] Compared to *Umbrella*, the exploding wire produced about a 10 orders of magnitude (10^{-10}) smaller yield, equivalent to about 1 gram of TNT.

To reproduce the bubble dynamics anticipated from kiloton underwater nuclear explosions (see Chapter 7), the atmosphere above the water in the tank had to be below ambient, and then only the first bubble expansion and contraction would emulate a nuclear bubble with acceptable accuracy. My colleagues and I wanted to determine the detonation product distribution inside a nuclear bubble when it reached its first maximum radius.

---

[61] Buntzen, R.R., 'The Use of Exploding Wires in the Study of Small-Scale Underwater Explosions," in *Exploding Wires, Volume 2*, ed. W.G. Chase and H.K. Moore, 245-263, Plenum Press, Ney York, 1962.

My research in underwater nuclear explosions using an exploding wire had begun a couple of years earlier, after returning from Hardtack I. In my sixth-floor lab, I'd constructed a small explosion tank, which could not sustain a vacuum above the water surface, but allowed me to work out the exploding wire circuitry and make the scaling calculations needed to build a larger facility on the first floor. At that time, other Navy laboratories employed small TNT charges in the small-scale simulations. My colleagues and I expected that the radionuclide distribution in the *Wahoo* and *Umbrella* base surge might be different from model TNT predictions, if the interior atmosphere of the underwater bubble condensed as it formed. We wanted to know how and why. Computer modeling of the phenomena was beginning and the measurements would help.

The pace of my work increased after moving the electronics to the first-floor explosion tank. I used a gold wire to initiate the underwater discharge and employed a probe with a small, cylindrical chamber that sealed on command, to sample the interior of the bubble at various radii when it reached its maximum. I wanted to obtain a radial distribution of wire residue. Each sample from the bubble interior was carefully washed into a small vial. After I collected a couple of dozen vials, I carried them to General Atomics Corporation in San Diego to undergo neutron activation. The resulting radiation levels gave me the number of gold wire atoms as a function of the bubble maximum radius.

During my experiments, I was also measuring the explosion energy that went to creating the bubble and the energy generating the shock wave. The Navy was interested in increasing the explosive energy partitioned into the shock wave for use against submarines and reducing the hazard from above-surface events caused by an energetic bubble. In other words, they wanted to make a better weapon. That was not my defense mission, but—I had an idea to do just that!

During the very early stage of the fireball, radiant energy escapes from the nuclear mass before the shock wave separates. I surmised that some of the radiant energy in the wavelength region that water transmitted (mostly visible part of the spectrum) did not participate in the formation of the shock front. If I could trap that energy closer to the vaporized wire, it might generate higher shockwave pressure and reduce the bubble size and resulting surface effects. My big idea was to place a thin glass tube filled with black ink tightly over the electrodes holding the wire so that the visible light would be absorbed inside and potentially create more shock energy. The necessary theoretical calculations were very difficult to make in those days, so I chose to do an experiment and measure the effects first.

I had asked our glass blower, Roy Bryant, to make a number of thin cylindrical shells that would slip over the electrodes and make a watertight seal. Roy initially had trouble making the shells thin enough not to disturb the explosion. It was taking longer than I wanted and I was getting anxious, building up the potential results of my idea in my mind. After several days of delay, I picked up the shells. It was near quitting time on Friday. Excited, I decided to decline a party invitation and stay at work to begin the series of measurements to verify any difference in explosion energy partition between the shock wave and bubble.

First, I placed a shell between the electrodes in the tank and filled it with India ink to absorb the visible radiant energy. I closed the glass access door and dogged it down tight. Next, I pumped filtered water into the explosion tank from a holding tank outside the north wall of Building 815. While the explosion tank was filling, I placed a roll of 35 mm film in the high-speed camera to capture the bubble expansion, and set the oscilloscope that monitored a piezoelectric gauge recording the pressure trace. Finally, I started the vacuum pump and threw the switch to charge the capacitor—but wait!

This is where I hit a wall. A subliminal thought forced its way into my consciousness. I stopped and waited, beginning to think about what I was actually doing. I was trying to unlock nature's secrets on how to make a better weapon! There did not seem to be any other use for the knowledge I was about to uncover. However, it was my job. But was it defense? Had I stumbled into the realm of weapon development I had so far avoided? Was I about to make a mistake? Would I be responsible for how the knowledge I found was used?

I had to know the answer. I somehow needed to know the answer to my energy partition question. I could not just walk away now. Or could I? I needed time to think.

I shut everything down and went to the party.

What party? I left after a few distracted interactions with some friends and others and raced back to the lab. Everything was dark and quiet. The gate guards were accustomed to late comings and goings, and the NRDL guard likewise thought it was ok for someone to come back to the lab late in the evening.

Still dressed in corduroy, I cranked everything up again and fired the first shot. The pressure trace looked the same—no change from earlier shots where there was water instead of ink in the sleeve. It took about an hour to pump out the water, open the tank door, reset the exploding wire and ink sleeve, and refill and pump down the tank for another shot. Again, no change. I tried a shot without the ink. No change in shockwave pressure resulted. Since I needed about a week to get the high-speed film developed, to see if there was a change in the bubble diameter indicating that less energy went into its formation, I finally quit for the night. Disappointed, but relieved as well, I went home. What had just happened?

After a restless sleep in the hour or so that remained before morning, I returned and fired several more ink shots, using up all of Roy's sleeves. I changed the capacitor bank voltage to vary the explosion yield, collected all the film, and sent it to the developer. Their service was fast, and it took only a couple of days before the film arrived back at the lab. As with the pressure trace, the films also showed that there was no change in the bubble maximum radius when the wire was surrounded with ink. The experiment was a failure! Maybe it never would have worked.

The experiment failed, but I gained a valuable insight into my basic nature. Even though I could not see any possible result of my experiment other than weapon-design improvement, the desire to know the answer trumped any moral conflict I felt. Did my curiosity overcome reason? In choosing to work in national defense, could I easily turn to weaponry and devise ways to kill people? Why was I so emotional that night?

Ultimately, I did believe there is a difference between defensive and offensive research work, and it made a difference to me in choosing a career path. I know that "the best defense is a good offense," but I prefer to work the defense side (although sometimes there is little difference), and I feel good about it. However, that night, I learned the power and lure of curiosity. The intellectual need to "know the answer" is extremely powerful—and I am susceptible to it.

Mission Accomplished

Mission accomplished? Really? There were rumors that NRDL might close! How could that happen? Had we fully addressed all the problems of nuclear warfare at sea? Had all the issues that radioactive nuclides generate when released on our troops and general population been exhaustively studied and all questions answered? What was going on?

It must have been sometime in mid-1966 that I began to hear about a weakening in NRDL's mission statement taking place in Washington, DC. Yes, the giant government bureaucratic gears were turning and there was pressure to reorganize the nation, including R&D, for more focus on the Vietnam War, and, oh yes, save money. Dr. Eugene Cooper, our technical director, was worried.

Fortunately, NRDL had recently formed a new Technology Management Office, under Paul Zigman, to assist Dr. Walmar (Jerry) Strope, director of research for the DOD's Office of Civil and Defense Mobilization in Washington, DC. The technical staff of Paul's group rapidly grew and expanded their scope to find new mission areas for NRDL that could attract sponsors. Several scientists were asked to join the new office with a broad charter to scout uses for our expertise.[62] I joined the Reconnaissance Technical Group, a unit in Paul's new organization.

NRDL fought back the trend by dispatching Paul Zigman, Bill Kreger, and Sam Rainey to Washington, DC, to lobby congressional

---

[62]   Zigman. P. review comments, December 2016.

representatives, high-ranking civilian and military people in the DOD, and the White House to keep the lab open. Toward the end of two weeks of campaigning in the halls of power, including meetings with a couple of Senators and Representatives who influenced nuclear energy work, Sam and Paul ended up in a meeting with the director of the Office of Science and Technology (OST). President John F. Kennedy had established OST in 1961, as a precursor of the current Office of Science and Technology Policy. Paul and Sam were excited, since they had been highly recommended after a meeting with the secretary of education and the request he forwarded to "listen to what they have to say." Dr. Vincent McRhae (OST) greeted them warmly, offered them coffee, and listened carefully to their pitch. Then he stood up and said, "You know, you've made a very interesting case. But—it's a no-go." That's when the lights went out for NRDL in Washington, DC.[63]

In Washington, NRDL's closure became "a reorientation within the Navy research and development establishment" in order for the "creation of large centers of excellence, each of sufficient size and technical capability to develop large and complex warfare systems. A study of NRDL's activities indicated that its mission, experience, and size were too confined to undertake major systems responsibilities. This activity is not a part of the major Navy acquisition programs. Further, even if in the unlikely event they could be involved in future major programs, the NRDL immediate locale and physical environment are unsuitable for increasing the magnitude of its operation."[64]

In other words, it was all over! We could do nothing to save our jobs. It was true that the Navy gained significant information on how to wash down ships and seal the interiors in case of exposure to a nuclear, biological, or chemical environment from our work. It was true that significant information on human reaction to exposure to radiation fields and how ingestion of radionuclides affected survival came from our work, etc. However, it was also true that by this time NRDL

[63] Ibid.
[64] Operational Archives, Naval Historical Center, Washington Navy Yard, Washington DC, Navy R&D Management Archive Collection #00006, Series 00010, Box 00707, March 1969, p. 1.

was not the only center that could carry out the research required in these areas. The larger military laboratories had begun parallel efforts during the previous decade of easy funding for such work, and civilian laboratories and universities had entered the nuclear radiation field of study. NRDL was no longer unique.

For me, this period with Paul's group, searching for new areas of funding to practice technical expertise, was both exciting and inspiring. We still thought there was a chance to save the laboratory and vigorously pursued the new technical challenge. During this time, I learned about laser and radar sensors for tactical warfare as they related the Vietnam War. Bob Hammond and I had the opportunity to travel to Yankee Station off North Vietnam aboard the USS Enterprise. I followed through in-country from Da Nang to the delta below Saigon to evaluate the use of side-looking radar for finding North Vietnamese missile and anti-aircraft artillery sites. I also became involved in the Navy's high-energy laser weapons program because of my experience in the thermal effects of nuclear weapons and in several other special projects associated with the Vietnamese war effort.

NRDL closed by official memorandum from its commanding officer, Capt. T.R. Fick, on July 24, 1969. The last days at NRDL were depressing. Our new CO was suspiciously optimistic, He'd arrived at NRDL sometime in mid-1968 during the trying discussions between our technical director, Dr. Cooper, the director of Navy laboratories, and other Washington sponsors. Captain Fick was privy to the decisions being made, but he assured us during an all-hands meeting in early '69 that NRDL was not going to close, along with the announcement that he had bought a house and was settling down for a long stay. (We later found out that he was retiring from the Navy and would remain in the area.) However, the gears continued to turn in Washington.

The NRDL disestablishment schedule was announced on April 24, 1969,[65] laying out the disestablishment teams, transfer plans, reduction in force numbers, equipment relocation plan, etc., and ending with the official disestablishment on December 25th. Imagine—Christmas

---

[65]   Ibid, p. 6.

Day! Closure of NRDL resulted in the loss of possibly the largest, most integrated research institution in the U.S. dedicated to understanding the effects of nuclear radiation.

Two hundred twenty scientific and technical personnel transferred to other Navy laboratories, and everyone else was fired. I considered the chance to transfer to the Naval Ordinance Laboratory in White Oak, Maryland, with 101 others. However, I didn't like that option and flew to San Diego to talk Dr. Bill McLean, the technical director of the Naval Undersea Weapons Center (NUWC) into a job. He had developed the Sidewinder air-to-air missile while at the Naval Ordnance Test Station-China Lake, California.

His reputation was so strong with the Navy and Congress that they gave him the bayside part of the Navy Electronics Laboratory on Point Loma, San Diego. Dr. McLean believed that the Navy needed a new undersea technology laboratory. Bob Hammond and I had a funded project in high-energy laser weapons, and Dr. McLean accepted us both as part of his technical staff. That was good luck because NOL, White Oak was closed a couple of years later and their research staff integrated into the Naval Weapons Laboratory in Dahlgren, Virginia. (I was happy to move to Southern California, since Mom and Dad still lived in Chula Vista, just south of San Diego.)

Sixty-three other employees received an offer to transfer to NUWC. Evan somehow talked Bill McLean into allowing him to transfer to NUWC's facility in Kaneohe Bay, Hawaii, to continue the work in marine biology he had begun after receiving his doctorate from Berkeley. Many of my colleagues declined the transfer offers and joined private companies or started their own businesses, preferring to stay in the San Francisco Bay Area. The Hunters Point Shipyard ceased operations in 1974 and officially closed through a Base Realignment and Closure Commission (BRAC) action in 1991. (The Navy is still involved in radiation cleanup activities associated with ground contamination during the attempt to deal with the radioactive ships from Operation Crossroads.)

The work done by all the military laboratories was beginning to change. Government laboratories were no longer block funded to respond to specific warfare problems or missions. In 1969, the Navy converted all its applied laboratories to Navy Industrial Funding, which meant that sponsorship was a free-for-all and the traditional lines of funding no longer mattered. In-house research supporting the development cycle was starting to drift away from government institutions to the contractors holding interest in the performance of their systems, thus reducing government oversight. The very formulation of what Navy war-fighting operations needed in combat began to shift to corporations that dreamed up, lobbied, built, and evaluated the systems they received funding to build.

Was the demise of NRDL an effective move for Navy research? Naturally, I am biased on this question. I remember too well the camaraderie, dedication to the mission, and intellectual excitement at NRDL. From 1969 on, I saw the Navy laboratories I knew die and change into management activities for large systems-acquisition contractors. No longer is there a place for small, dedicated, highly integrated government organizations that concentrated on a research problem area. This is a shame, mainly because it is only with such a concentration of the expertise required that the government can monitor and evaluate what for-profit contractors are selling.

Maybe NRDL was a good example of how applied research at the national level should be done: identify the mission (radiological defense), organize and focus the assets in a single laboratory (NRDL), generously fund the critical effort (block funding, no lobbying, politicking and marketing), and then disestablish the activity when the mission is accomplished—or fails. But it hurt, and still does.

For years, I wondered what happened to the NRDL building, Building 815, after it closed. Recently, returning along Highway 101 from the 2013 NRDL reunion, I looked again at the old laboratory building that stood to the east, across a shallow basin adjacent to Candlestick Stadium. Often when traveling south from San Francisco, I would take a long look at the building. Sometimes it stood bright in sunlight, in high contrast against the decaying remains of the Hunters Point Shipyard. Other times it appeared as a grey, ghostly structure, almost lost in the haze and low-lying fog that often settled over the area.

If not maintained, the interior of Building 815 would quickly turn into a rusted, useless mess. Feeling rather saddened by the small turnout for the reunion, it was time to visit Building 815.

The Base Realignment and Closure Commission maintains a liaison office in San Francisco to oversee the remaining Navy portion of the shipyard and land turned over to the city for commercial development. A call to the office led me to Iron Mountain, a records storage company, and a local phone number. Iron Mountain is a multi-billion dollar, international company that specializes in data backup and records management and storage. In 1997, it needed more space for paper file storage and leased Building 815 from its earlier owner, who had bought it through auction from the Government Services Administration in the mid-1980s. Iron Mountain needed a large vault to safely store paper files and records—and got a good one. Repurposing the building for its current use was complete shortly after the purchase.

A phone call to Iron Mountain led to my visit and a nostalgic but bittersweet experience. My old entry route on Crisp Road dead-ended, redirecting me to Third Avenue and down Evans Avenue on a torturous path leading through the remains of the shipyard. The empty, crumbling buildings humming with activity when NRDL flourished sadly reminded me of all my colleagues' lives that changed on December 25, 1969. As I approached Building 815, stress cracks in the faded grey walls became visible, briefly taking my thoughts away from the unmaintained, junk-laden surrounding areas. I met the Iron Mountain site manager and signed the visitor log. Several small offices displaying old photos of the building and surrounding shipyard served as a spare waiting area for visitors.

I wanted to see my explosion tank research lab on the first floor, since it held so many of my fondest memories of NRDL. Today, all the interior walls are gone and only the concrete support pillars provide a foundation for the upper floors. Eight-foot-high iron racks holding thousands of boxes full of paper files create partitions between access aisles. Every indication that my large explosion tank existed is gone. My sadness deepened.

Next, I wanted to see my sixth-floor office/laboratory, where I spent hours, days, and months building instruments and analyzing data. The interior escalators I flew up and down on between floors are gone, so we took the north service elevator. Exiting, I faced a mirror image of the first-floor racks and boxes (Fig. 23). All the sophisticated chemistry labs are gone, as are the bio labs on the fifth floor. We walked to the building's north end, where the large auditorium used to be. More boxes covered the sloping floor and stage foundation remains. Only the projection box remained to indicate that the room had once been an auditorium. I walked to the stage area and recalled the hours practicing presentations as well as presenting some for the technical director's lecture series.

My Iron Mountain host and another worker related rumors the employees had heard about the "old" laboratory: the building was haunted and radioactive monkeys sometimes bounded between racks of boxes late at night. And the military head of the laboratory had been a health nut, making the scientists do exercises. He even removed all the chairs from the cafeteria on the roof above, maintaining that it was healthier to stand during lunch and coffee breaks. Iron Mountain employees in the past have shown ghost images from the projection box and played spooky music for Halloween, underscoring the haunted theme. I assured them that all the monkeys used in the fifth-floor experiments were gone and that the cafeteria did have chairs. However, I couldn't resist telling them that there was rumor of a higher-than-normal suicide rate associated with NRDL.

On the way out, we walked by the stairs that provided the only access we could use for the cafeteria. It was blocked, the rooftop cafeteria and equipment associated with the labs having been removed long ago. The personnel from Iron Mountain were very gracious, and I appreciate the time they took to satisfy my curiosity about what happened to the unique laboratory. Today, there are few productive activities on the remaining shipyard land: a University of California San Francisco environmental monitoring station, a commercial wood mill, and Building 815. As I drove home, my sadness lifted, knowing that my old laboratory building was still alive.

AFTERWORD

Was *Oak* really an Armageddon experience? Although my exposure to *Oak* during the Hardtack I test series at Enewetak holds a special place in my memory, the same isn't true for some of my colleagues who had previously witnessed several high-megaton detonations. During interviews and correspondence with Evan, Tak, and Dick Soule, all who had participated in earlier test series, I found that they remembered *Oak* as having noticeably greater thermal and shock effects, but they did not see the event as an Armageddon experience. Even Roger Caputi and Walt Gurney now look back on the effects of *Oak* as being impressive, but not the overwhelming event that I do.

I was curious. Were there others who had witnessed *Oak* from a similar close-in vantage point, either from Enewetak Island or aboard an observation ship? Were there other nuclear test participants from other nuclear test operations who had similar experiences? What did they report? What do they now remember?

To some extent, it may have been my later career training in operations research and systems analysis that led me to see *Oak* as I described: the face of Armageddon. Even though the danger that nuclear weapons threatened interested me while at NRDL, my later work in military operations and advanced technology widened my understanding of the enormous power I had witnessed. I need only look back at the U.S. fallout maps predicted from a hypothesized Soviet attack to realize that *Oak* could create the experience of a real Armageddon.

For some who witnessed multiple multi-megaton detonations over a period of several years as part of the nuclear weapons test series, there may be a familiarization effect. We find it with many experiences that are more common. However, I don't think so. It would be regrettable to ever lose the first impressions gained from experiencing a nearby nuclear detonation and learn to take an event of such horrendous force as commonplace, or as an option for any possible disagreement between nations. I prefer to believe that the reason my colleagues have forgotten the physical impact of *Oak* comes from their desire never to think about such things after NRDL closed. Their reaction is understandable.

My research found few accounts from other Hardtack I participants who might have seen *Oak* from a distance of 20 miles or less. A notable exception is Walter E. Venator, who participated in Operation Hardtack I and has created a web document that includes *Oak* eyewitness stories from military personnel.[66] From his account, George Mace, an Air Force enlisted man assigned to JTF-7 in communications maintenance, gave the following description of *Oak* from a location on Fred (Enewetak) Island:[67]

> When OAK detonated, there was this wink of light that I sensed through my closed eyes and arms, just like a flashbulb going off inside my head. And when I turned to see the column of water rising out of the lagoon, it was so tremendous that no one spoke. You could hear the sound waves bouncing off the islands Boom! Boom!, as it came down the atoll chain. And when the sound wave hit Eniwetok, the whole island shook and a hot wind blew our baseball caps off, but within seconds the wind reversed and sucked in toward the bomb. The column was surrounded by ragged haloes of white shock waves, which produced an electrical field. I actually experienced an electrical field passing through me; my arm hair stood up and there was a cracking sensation all through

66   Venator, Walter E., Jr., *Where the Boys Were, Hardtack 1, 1958*, 2011, full text web download, http://home.us.archive.org/stream/WhereTheBoysWere/WheretheBoysWere_djvu.txt.

67   Ibid, p. 25.

me that was as much felt as heard. I knew what this was because I had felt the same effect when in the field of a high-powered radio antenna. There was also a metallic taste in my mouth, like when chewing gum foil touches a tooth filling.

And that mushroom cloud just continued to build and grow until it had risen about sixty or seventy thousand feet into the air and covered the entire atoll. A circle of islands about fifteen miles in diameter were all shadowed by this terrifying, magnificent thing. I remember talk of evacuating the islands because of concern about fallout, but it never occurred. After fifteen or twenty minutes, the water in the lagoon began to recede until the lagoon bottom lay exposed for about two hundred yards from shore. I could see sunken PT boats and equipment from WWII that was normally covered by fifteen or twenty feet of water. I really thought the earth had cracked and that the water was running into it! I mean, it had to go somewhere, right? Finally, the water stopped receding and it just stood there like a wall for a minute. I thought of Moses and the parting of the Red Sea, for it must have looked like this! Then it started coming back and I got a sick feeling, because here I was on this dinky little island, not very wide, and here comes what seemed like the whole ocean. The wave hit the island and sprayed up over the sandbags and all day long the water kept seesawing back and forth. Because of this agitation, the lagoon water turned an ugly milk chocolate brown and it started to rain very hard. At this point, the effects of the bomb detonation took on an apocalyptic gloom and I felt oppressed! Prometheus had stolen heavens fire and Pandora's Box spilled a Nuclear Holocaust on mankind forever! The bomb had created a column, which sucked up all the lagoon water for fifteen miles around. I will never forget that. The lagoon water was off limits for swimming for three days, but the ironic part of it was that the lagoon was our source of drinking water, after it went through the desalinization plant, which did not remove radiation. The mighty OAK had dug a crater 183 feet deep in the lagoon and 4,400 feet in diameter. It also made a good size dent in my memory bank!

I do not remember feeling an electromagnetic pulse of energy or the hair on my arms standing up, but it is more than a coincidence that George Mace also thought of Moses when he saw the wall of water. Tadd Kowalzyk, Det25, 15th Weather Squadron, provided a similar account in Venator's document as a weather observer conducting upper-air balloon flights that helped predict and track the fallout from a detonation.[68]

> Oak was a 9.8-megaton yield hydrogen bomb that was detonated in I think June 8 on the NNW side of the lagoon 24 1/2 miles from the island of Fred. The shot left a crater in solid rock 1500 feet deep and 5 miles in diameter. The mushroom cloud rose to a height of 200,000 feet as seen by our CPS9 weather radar which was located near the base operations building on a tower about 80 feet high. Our weather balloons could only average about 100,000 feet altitude and the upper flow was to the NE, which means we should have been safe from fallout. The upper level of the cloud sheared off and moved SSE and some landed on Fred and Japtan. For Oak, I and those of my unit not directly at work, were in formation facing away from the blast with left arms over our eyes wearing long leg and sleeve fatigues. At detonation, I could see the outline of my barracks across the road and felt an instant 'sunburn' to my neck and back as well as the back facing portion of my ears. We were told not to look at the blast until the count got back to 10 but at 4 I snuck a look with my left eye covered. I was only 19 and still not very smart and paid for it with dead spots on my optic nerve, which are there to this date. Through the miracle of binocular vision and the brain filling the blank spots I still have 20/20 vision.

There may be other firsthand close-in accounts of Shot *Oak* or other multi-megaton yield detonations now beginning to surface on the internet. Unfortunately, many of the personal stories found in Venator's work are from victims of unfortunate situations during nuclear tests.

---

[68]   Ibid, p. 29.

The Atomic Veterans of America keeps a record of those assigned to jobs that apparently resulted in their receiving harmful levels of radiation.

Several tests during Operation Hardtack I, as in the preceding Operation Redwing, demonstrated that a smaller amount of long-lived radionuclides result when the fission process initiating the neutron-rich fusion reaction is reduced. (I do not think that Soviet weapon designs considered this option when generating the fallout patterns used by OCDM, thereby maximizing the potential fallout hazard.) Sometime after returning from Enewetak, I heard about a U.S. effort through the United Nations to demonstrate a "clean" fusion weapon during Hardtack I. A number of foreign observers were invited to observe Hardtack I *Piñon*, a 4.5 MT water surface detonation based on earlier Operation Redwing devices. *Piñon* would demonstrate a 5% fission yield, allowing 95% of the total yield to be from fusion reactions.[69]

Careful measurement of the *Piñon* fireball diameter would provide an accurate measurement of the *Piñon* total yield. The fission contribution is determined through radiochemistry by determining the number of fissions taking place in fallout sample containing a U_3O_8 tracer. The UN observation team would have attended briefings in Berkeley then flown to Enewetak to observe the test from Parry Island. Although less than half the yield of *Oak*, the demonstration would have been impressive. Unfortunately, *Piñon* did not take place, allegedly due to the accidental death of its technical director, Dr. Mark Mills, in a helicopter crash while at Hardtack I. In addition, the Soviets had refused the invitation to attend.

It is obvious that the first close-in exposure to a high-yield nuclear detonation produces a significant response that does not easily go away. It seemed to me like *Piñon* might have served as a reminder of what horror was possible if nuclear war broke out, beyond any consideration of how "clean" the nuclear assembly was. Soviet planners were already experienced in what their weapons could do, and it is not surprising that they declined the invitation to witness *Piñon*. Other foreign invitations

69   Johnson, Gerald, *Handbook for United Nations Observers, Piñon Test, Eniwetok,* UCRL 5367, Deleted Version, 1994.

ended up canceled, or declined, and the idea of a demonstration detonation was forgotten.

I remember thinking that the U.S. had missed a great opportunity. If political leaders from around the world could have the sensual experience I did, they would see beyond the cold science and politics and have a better grasp of the dangers of nuclear war. The thought seems as relevant today as it did then.

As for *Oak*—yes, for me it was an Armageddon experience, but incomparable to the events witnessed by the population of Hiroshima and Nagasaki. I cannot imagine that horror.

The Fate of the Marshallese

Recreating the events that I experienced on Enewetak and Parry Islands for this memoir led me to wonder what the overall impact of the nuclear tests was on the people inhabiting Enewetak and Bikini Atolls, as well as what the islands are like today. Clearly, massive alterations in the physical structure of the tiny islands and radioactive fallout created by the many nuclear detonations would have long-term effects on the Marshallese, societies that had inhabited the islands long before the U.S. decided to conduct atomic tests in their backyard. Although Rongelap and other smaller atolls in the Pacific Proving Grounds received serious contamination from radioactive fallout from Castle *Bravo*, I have limited my curiosity to the two atolls I became familiar with through my experience on Parry Island.

The Bikinians. Bikini Atoll lies far off the normal shipping routes, surrounded by a vast open ocean supporting few native groups on scattered atolls. The Navy thoroughly scoured the Marshall Islands for a suitable test area and chose Bikini Atoll. The problem was the Bikinians. They inhabited the atoll islands and required relocation. In March 1946, all 167 of them were ferried to Rongerik Atoll.

The discussions between the U.S. Navy and the Bikinians began pleasantly enough. The Navy had saved the people of Bikini from what had become an oppressive relationship with the Japanese, and a friendly relationship had developed between the two current but disparate cultures. Soon after President Truman announced that Bikini Atoll would be the testing grounds for the newly developed atomic weapons, Commodore Ben H. Wyatt, the military governor of the Marshall Islands, flew to Bikini Island. On a Sunday after church in February 1946, he assembled the Bikinians to ask if they would be willing to temporarily leave their atoll so that the United States could begin testing atomic bombs for "the good of mankind and to end all world wars." King Juda, leader of the Bikinian people, stood up after much confused and sorrowful deliberation among his people and announced, "We will go believing that everything is in the hands of God."[70] What resulted is still a nightmare for the Bikinians.

Lying about 200 miles east of Bikini, the 17 islands making up Rongerik Atoll are 1/6 the size of Bikini Atoll, devoid of adequate food and water supplies, and at the time thought by the Marshallese to be inhabited by evil spirits. By early 1947, the Bikinians were literally starving to death, requiring the Navy to move them from Rongerik to survive. During this time, the U.S. was given the Marshall Islands as a strategic trust by the United Nations with the stipulation to "promote the economic advancement and self-sufficiency of the inhabitants and to this end shall...protect the inhabitants against the loss of their lands and resources."[71]

Receiving considerable criticism from the international community for this treatment, the U.S. decided to move the Bikinians to Ujilang Atoll, which would offer better living conditions. But that too became a problem, since Ujilang was to be offered to the Enewetakese since their Atoll had just been selected as an additional nuclear weapons test site. Ujilang Atoll lies southeast, closer to Enewetak and consists of a land mass of only 0.8 square miles—far too small to support both native populations. The Bikinians had to remain on Rongerik until March

---

[70] Niedenthal, Jack, *A Short History of the People of Bikini Atoll*, Updated August, 2010. http://www.bikiniatoll.com/.

[71] Ibid.

1948. They remained there and suffered near starvation for two years before moving into tents erected for them in a secured area on Kwajalein Island, then to Kili Island in the southern Marshalls three months later.

The move to Kili Island was a decision made by the Bikinians, primarily because the island was inhabited and they would not be subjected to rule by the king of another native group. Kili is an island of less than 0.4 square miles of landmass and does not have a lagoon, which was the source of abundant fish in their Bikini Atoll homeland. The surrounding seas were difficult to fish, and some months of the year, fishing is altogether impossible. Nor could the island produce enough copra to support the needs of 184 people. At times over the following years, food was so scarce that supplies were air-dropped to again fend off starvation. The proud and independent Bikinians had made a decision that adversely impacts them still. Today, the population of Kili is about 600, primarily descendants of the original Bikinians. They still resupply on a regular basis to survive.

In 1956, the Bikinians received an agreement from the U.S. for the continued use of Kili Island, the right to return to Bikini Atoll after the weapons test program ended, and $25,000 in cash and a trust fund of $300,000, paying a semi-annual interest of $15.00 per person. Within a couple of years after the Limited Test Ban Treaty in 1963, the radiation damage many of the Marshallese on other islands received was becoming apparent, and treatment, compensation, and radioactivity cleanup activities on Bikini and Enewetak expanded. The Bikinians had not received a serious radioactive exposure from the fallout and appear to have been forgotten in comparison to those who had identifiable medical problems from being in harm's way.

The Bikinians struggled to survive throughout the nuclear weapons test period, with inadequate sustenance support from the U.S., until 1972, when they returned to Bikini. The atoll had undergone radiological clean-up, foliage restoration, and housing construction. The Atomic Energy Commission announced that coconut crabs found in the Bikini lagoon were safe to eat on a limited (not regular) basis. By the end of 1974, nearly half of the Bikinians living on Kili Island had moved back to Bikini. They expected to return to the lifestyle they remembered, and they remembered the promises the Navy had made to them.

However, in 1975, additional radiation-monitoring studies showed that the remaining radiological contamination exceeded acceptable levels of long-term exposure. The Bikinians sued the U.S. to conduct a complete radiological survey of the atoll and carry out a more rigorous clean-up.[72] While the U.S. dawdled over the lawsuit, surveys showed that the Bikinians' radiation levels exceeded safe levels, and the population was yet again relocated. For some reason, the cleanup of Enewetak was much more intense and organized than that conducted on Bikini, where it seemed to be more of a study than an actual remediation effort.

By 1977, tests showed that the people living on Bikini were ingesting high levels of cancer-causing radionuclides. The U.S. began sending nearly all the food and liquids people required to Bikini. In 1978, tests identified additional radioactive sources and even higher potential exposure to radiation from any consumable produced on the island. By August that year, all Bikinians living on the atoll returned to Kili. It seems that they did not escape the fallout from the weapons tests after all. Bikini remained off limits for long-term habitation, and the radioactivity surveys continued. In 1992, the atoll opened as an underwater dive destination for those wishing to tour the remains of the Operation Crossroads' target fleet.

The lawsuit continued until March 2001, when the Nuclear Claims Tribunal handed the Bikinians an award of $563,000 for damages. Unfortunately, the government organization charged with paying the damages was underfunded and unable to meet the obligation, requiring the Bikinians to petition Congress for distribution of the money. The U.S. Supreme Court turned down the lawsuit in 2006, and the Bikinians sued again. In 2010, the U.S. Supreme Court refused to revisit the case.

Later that year, the World Heritage Committee inscribed the Bikini Atoll Nuclear Test Site on the World Heritage List, for the role that tests of atomic weapons at Bikini played in shaping global culture in the second half of the 20th Century. Today, the Bikinians are scattered

---

[72]   https://en.wikipedia.org/wiki/Bikini_Atoll#Trust_funds_and_failed_claims.

throughout the Marshall Islands, still awaiting funds to clean up Bikini, so they can again live in their homeland. In March 2012, a delegation from Bikini Atoll made up of the mayor, congressional representative, and trust fund representative met with U.S. congressional representatives to discuss the status of the authorized resettlement funds, which are still unpaid.

The Bikinians continue to raise funds for their cleanup through tourism, dive trips, and boat tours, all based out of Kwajalein Island. Dive trips and tours, which are the source of funds assisting their remediation efforts, are advertised on the web, along with an address for donations.

The Enewetakese. Thirty MT of nuclear energy were released on the islands making up Enewetak Atoll in the ten-year testing period.[73] One-third of the total energy released was during a single detonation, Operation Ivy, Shot *Mike*, the first U.S. thermonuclear device. The insult to Enewetak Atoll resulted in the obliteration of Elugelab Island from that single detonation, and the radioactive contamination of the coral and foliage on most of the northern atoll islands.

The total yield released on Enewetak Atoll over the years grew rapidly as thermonuclear devices were developed. Operation Sandstone, 1948, resulted in the release of 104 KT; Operation Greenhouse, 1951, 400 KT; Operation Ivy, 1952, 10,900 KT; Operation Castle, 1954, 1,700 KT (single detonation at Enewetak); Operation Redwing, 1956, 2,555 KT; and Operation Hardtack, 1958, 14,557 KT. Most of the detonations were staged on the islands directly north and to the northwest of Parry Island over the years, Runit Island apparently taking the greatest number of hits. Engebi hosted ten detonations. Aomon −3, Runit −17, Eberiru −2, Elugelab −2 (1 in the Mike crater), Bogon −2, Rujoru −1, Flora−1, and Bokoluo −1.

Before World War II, the Enewetakese consisted of two clans known as the riEnewetak (the people of Enewetak Island) and the

---

[73]   http://www10.antenna.nl/wise/index.html?http://www10.antenna.nl/wise/454
/4498.html.

riEnjebi (the people of Enjebi Island). Because of their isolation from the richer southern atolls preferred by the early colonists, they were the last in the Marshallese influenced by missionaries and had developed a strong and an almost mystical attachment to their land.

During the American campaign against the Japanese, both Enewetak and Enjebi Islands, (unlike Bikini, which retained its pristine environment during the war), were almost entirely denuded of foliage and almost 10% of the Enewetakese killed, forcing those who would not leave to move to two small islands along the eastern side of the atoll. They remained there throughout World War II while the Americans rebuilt and occupied their original homelands.

In late 1947, Enewetak was chosen as a weapons test site, and the surviving Enewetakese moved to Ujilang in place of the Bikinians, who were scheduled to move there from their displaced home on Rongerik. A much smaller atoll than Enewetak, life on Ujilang was exceedingly difficult for the Enewetakese over the next 30 years.

After much haggling with the Americans to return to their homeland, and a series of mutinies with the Marshallese governing administration, the Bikinians had experienced some success, and in 1972, some of them were finally returning home. Enewetakese wanted to follow suit. However, radiological surveys revealed that some islands of Enewetak Atoll, more heavily contaminated by radioactive debris than previously thought, would not be habitable for decades. In 1976, after extensive radiological surveys, it was determined that Enewetak Island and several others on the atoll's eastern rim could be partially restored with "reasonable safety." In this situation, "reasonable safety" referred to the residual level of radioactivity. Soil that exceeded 400 pCi (4×10^{-10}) of residual plutonium isotopes per gram had to be removed, while less contaminated soil could be amended, depending on the planned land-use. Apparently, some living situations could tolerate levels below 40 pCi (10^{-12} Ci).

The U. S. Congress provided funds for land cleanup, and a full-scale effort began in late 1977. The Enewetakese were consulted in the cleanup planning, and some were employed to help with the work. Efforts on Enewetak called for removing nearly all equipment, concrete, and other debris associated with the weapons test and either removing or amending all the soil with radiation readings above the acceptable level. The radioactive material amounted to an estimated 73,000 cubic meters of surface soil across six different atoll islands.

The contaminated material was mixed with Portland cement and buried in the blast crater from Hardtack I *Cactus* (5 MT), located at the northern end of Runit Island on the eastern side of the atoll. This work continued until the crater became a spherical mound 25 feet high. Finally, the mound was covered with an 18-inch thick concrete cap, dubbed "Cactus Dome" (Fig. 24), at a cost of $240 million. The cleanup of Enewetak Atoll soil, the construction of dwellings and community buildings, and an extensive replanting was complete by 1980. Some Enewetakese would not wait and began returning to the atoll before the cleanup was complete.

Currently, the U.S. has no formal custodial responsibilities for Cactus Dome and maintains that no contamination is escaping from the site. Today, there are no guard fences, and a visitor can walk up the shallow incline to the top of the dome. The dome is deteriorating, and over the remainder of the century, sea level rise will increase the potential of Pu^{239} remains of unexploded devices under the dome finding their way into the lagoon. Even though Pu isotopes from the Marshall Islands have been detected in the China Sea, nearly three thousand miles away, the Department of Energy claims that a catastrophic release of the dome contents is not a worry.[74]

Daily life on Enewetak appears relatively normal. In 2001, construction of the Enewetak Radiological Laboratory (ERL) to permanently monitor radiation level and its impact on the Enewetakese was completed and is permanently staffed by the Lawrence Livermore National Laboratory.[75] ERL's responsibility is to accurately track and assess doses delivered from ingested fallout contamination. Specialized whole-body radiation counters and spectrometers are located in ERL

---

[74]   Gerrard, Michael B., December 4, 2014, New York Times editorial.

[75]   A.A., R.E. Martinelli, K. Johannes, and D. Henry, *Individual Radiation Protection Monitoring in the Marshall Islands: Enewetak Atoll (2002-2004)*, UCRL-TR-220591, May 2006.

facilities conveniently located throughout the Marshall Islands for periodic measurement surveys to monitor and identify any radiation level changes.

***

Our government made many mistakes while conducting the nuclear weapons tests at the Pacific Proving Grounds. Technical mistakes are more familiar and understandable to me because of my particular training than the human ones I found while writing this section of my memoir. While I understand how an error in predicting a weapon yield might occur, I do not understand why the Bikinians still cannot return to their homeland. I do not understand why people on Rongelap were exposed to fallout for so long a time after Castle *Bravo*, or why the people aboard the *Lucky Dragon* had to fight so hard for compensation for what we did to them. The cost and effort to atone for these mistakes seems so small compared to the cost and labor put into the weapons tests that I do not understand why the Marshallese are still made to suffer.

It is sad that our government treats the Marshallese people so poorly. They gave up their homelands to help us avoid the very Armageddon effects we forced them to suffer. They gave so much that it is both unjust and immoral that we still neglect to honor their sacrifice. In addition, now they face another threat—a rising sea. As for the Bikinians, Bob Hope summed it all up well: "We located the one spot on Earth that hadn't been touched by the war and blew it to hell."[76]

---

[76] http://www.washingtonpost.com/sf/national/2015/11/27/a-ground-zero-forgotten.

ACRONYMS

ASROC   Antisubmarine Rocket

ASTOR   Antisubmarine Torpedo

AVR   Air Vehicle Rescue

CEP   Circular Error Probability

Ci   Curies, unit of radioactive decay rate; 1 Ci=3.7×10^{10} disintegrations per second

DOD   Department of Defense

DEFCON   Defense Readiness Condition

DUKW   Small amphibious landing craft (not an acronym)

FP   Film pack, free-floating and moored

GITOUT   GITR tape readout instrumentation

GITR   Gamma-Intensity-Time Recorder

H&N   Holmes and Narver Construction, Inc

IFC   Incremental Fallout Collector

JTF   Joint Task Force (Navy)

k, meV   Thousand/million electron volts

KT   Kilotons (equivalent to 10^3 tons of TNT)

LASL   Los Alamos Scientific Laboratory, currently Los Alamos National Laboratory

LCM/LCU   Landing Craft Mechanized/Utility

MATLAB®   MatrixLab, a commercial mathematical computing software developed by MathWorks

MATS   Military Air Transport Service

MT   Megatons (equivalent to 10^6 tons of TNT)

NCO   Noncommissioned Officers

NOL   Naval Ordnance Laboratory

NRDL   Naval Radiological Defense Laboratory

NUWC   Naval Underwater Weapons Laboratory

OCDM	Office of Civil and Defense Mobilization
OST(P)	Office of Science and Technology(Policy), established in 1961 by President John F Kennedy)
R, R/hr	Roentgen (electronic charge per unit of weight) dose and dose rate
rad	Radiation absorbed dose (energy per unit of weight, i.e. 100 ergs/gm)
rem	Radiation equivalent man
SBC	Sonoma Beach Club
Sv	Sievert (1 millisievert (mSv) = 100 millirem (mrem))
UC/UCLA	University of California at Berkeley/University of California at Los Angeles
UCRL	University of California Radiation Laboratory
UERL	Underwater Explosive Research Laboratory
USC	University of Southern California

TABLES

Operation (year)	Detonations (#)/ Total operation yield (KT)	Detonation Type(s)	Purpose(s)
Crossroads (1946)	(1) air drop, (1) underwater/ 46	Both fission, Mk 3A Fat Man, Pu core	Determine effects on ships, personnel, and material
Sandstone (1948)	(3) surface/ 104	Fission, new core designs	Improve fission efficiency
Greenhouse (1951)	(4) surface/ 388	Boosted fission core First fusion demonstration	Improve fission efficiency and test fusion core design
Ivy (1952)	(2) surface/ >10,000	First megaton fusion design/ Improved fission design	Basic physics and design confirmation
Castle (1954)	(6) surface/ >48,000	Improved fusion designs	Simpler, much smaller design validation for weapon
Redwing (1956)	(17) (1) airdrop, various surface/ > 20,000	(6) fusion greater than 1 MT, various core and initiation designs	First airdrop of a thermonuclear weapon. Other prototype design validation testing
Hardtack 1 (1958)	(35) high altitude, various surface and underwater/ >14,180	Fission and fusion assemblies. See Table 2 for more detail	Wide range of developmental, prototype and operational warhead design validation testing

Table 1. Pacific Proving Grounds nuclear weapon test operations, detonation types, and test objectives [summary of information found in https://enwikipedia.org/wiki/ (specificoperations) and nuclearweaponsarchive.org/USA/ tests/(specific operations)].

Shot name	Yield (KT)	Local time, 1958 date	Location/type	Device/warhead type,	
Organization	**Comments**				
Yucca	1.7	1440 April 28	NW, En., high altitude	W-25 ABM, AFSWP	From balloon,
Cactus	18	0615 May 6	En., surface	Mk-43 mock-up, LASL	LASL
Fir	1360	May 12	Bi., barge	Developmental, UCRL	
Butternut	81	May 12	En., barge	TX-46 developmental, LASL	
Koa	1370	May 13	En., surface	XW-35 ICBM warhead, LASL	
Wahoo	**9**	**May 16**	**En., underwater**	**MK-7 depth bomb, AFSWP**	
Holly	5.9	May 21	En., barge	XW-31Y3 proof test, LASL	
Nutmeg	25.1	May 21	Bi., barge	Xw-47 prototype, UCRL	
Yellowwood	330	1400 May 26	En., barge	TX-46 developmental, LASL	2.5 MT fizzle
Magnolia	57	May 27	En., barge	Developmental, LASL	
Tobacco	11.6	May 30	En., barge	Developmental, LASL	175 KT fizzle
Sycamore	92	May 31	Bi., barge	TX-41 warhead, UCRL	5 MT fizzle
Rose	15	June 3	En., barge	Developmental, LASL	fizzle
Umbrella	**8**	**1115 June 9**	**En., underwater**	**MK-7 depth bomb, AFSWP**	
Maple	213	June 11	Bi., barge	Developmental, UCRL	
Aspen	319	June 15	Bi., barge	XW-47 prototype, UCRL	
Walnut	1.5	June 15	En., barge	Developmental, LASL	
Linden	11	June 18	En., barge	Developmental, LASL	
Redwood	412	June 28	Bi., barge	Developmental, UCRL	
Elder	880	June 28	En., barge	TX-43 bomb, LASL	
Oak	8,900	0730 June 29	En., barge	TX-46 developmental, LASL	7,500 predicted
Hickory	14	June 29	Bi., barge	Developmental, UCRL	
Sequoia	5.2	July 2	En., barge	Developmental, LASL	
Cedar	220	July 3	Bi., barge	Developmental, UCRL	
Dogwood	397	July 6	En., barge	XW-47 prototype, UCRL	
Poplar	9,300	July 12	Bi., barge	TX-41 warhead, UCRL	
Scaevola	0	July 14	En., barge	Developmental,	Safety test

Pisonia	255	July 18	En., barge	XW-50 TN prototype, LASL	
Juniper	65	1620 July 22	Bi., barge	W-47 developmental, UCRL	Polaris warhead
Olive	202	July 23	En., barge	Developmental, UCRL	
Pine	2,000	July 27	En., barge	TX-41 warhead, UCRL, UCRL	
Teak	3,800	July 31	Johnson Isl., high altitude	ABM W-39 warhead, AFSWP	Redstone missile
Quince	0	August 2	En., surface	XW-51 developmental, AFSWP	Fizzle
Orange	3,800	August 11	Johnson Isl., high altitude	ABM W-39 warhead, AFSWP	Redstone missile
Fig	.02	August 18	En., surface	XW-51 developmental, AFSWP	successful

Table 2. Operation Hardtack I nuclear detonations (En. - Enewetak, Bi. - Bikini, AFSWP - Armed Services Special Weapons Project, UCRL - University of California Radiation Laboratory, LASL - Los Alamos Research Laboratory). Developmental refers to component or near-prototype device test. http://nuclearweaponarchive.org/Usa/Tests/ Hardtack1.html (accessed July 2011), and "Technical summary of Military Effects Programs 1-9," Operation Hardtack Preliminary Report, (1959), Interim Technical Report sanitized version (1999). Shots shown shaded were conducted during my stay on Parry Island.

APPENDIX DATA COLLECTION
AND ANALYSIS

Data Collection

To date, NRDL's is the most complete database for underwater nuclear weapon effects research in existence. Sparse instrumentation during the later *Swordfish* deep-water detonation resulted in little contribution to the Hardtack I radiation-hazard database.

Preliminary reports of field research projects typically contain a complete listing of the data collected, collection procedures, and an assessment of their quality, while highlighting any problems experienced. Examples of the data records are usually included and some initial conclusions drawn—usually with the appropriate caveats, and a pledge for refinements and recommendations to be completed for the final report. Before they left Parry, Evan and Tak provided Project 2.3 sponsors (the DOD and its Operation Hardtack I management agency, JTF-7) with copies of a large, bound document, containing a full description of the Project 2.3 preparation phase, execution, and copious diagrams of instruments, their positions, and example data records. There are preliminary conclusions and recommendations that remain classified in the interim report.

The primary instrument platforms were the coracles and destroyers containing the above and below water GITRs, IFCs, and FPs I described in Chapter 7. During *Wahoo*, the array-arming signal error resulted in collecting only 60% of the maximum possible data from the coracles (Fig. 16) and radio-controlled instruments aboard the ships. Much to my surprise, no significant data resulted from the individual free-floating FPs on *Wahoo*. (From now on, I will refer to the free-floating film packs as ffFPs.)

Overall test success was still judged good, not by the total amount of data collected but by considering its importance in mapping the radiological base surge movement. For example, the data from a distant coracle (e.g. coracle CL 60, Fig. 18) had lower significance if the wind took the base surge in another direction. In addition, if a coracle received little or no data relative to a coracle that recorded the full arrival and passage of the base surge, it played a smaller role when mapping the overall radiological event. The reason for over-designing a data-collection plan became clear.

Fortunately, nine of the 12 critical *Wahoo* stations provided good data, even though they received hurried and rough handling during the nighttime rearming operations. A power failure aboard two of the destroyers just prior to detonation resulted in their GITRs and IFCs failing to record any data. The arming-signal error and power loss aboard the destroyers were not associated with our project and illustrate some of the difficulties faced when participating in a large field test where much of the responsibility and control resides among more than one organization.

During *Wahoo*, the coracle physical problems were primarily due to mooring failures in the 5,000-plus foot deep water outside the atoll. Examination of the only deep mooring recovered due to time constraints showed a pure tension break in the cable from the 1,500-pound bottom weight and its grapnel to the coracle. In spite of the careful marine engineering design and added safety factors, some exceptional force, or combination of forces, occurring naturally and from the detonation, exceeded the mooring design limits. This caused some of the coracles to break loose and drift, during and after the radiological cloud passage, introducing coracle position errors during data analysis. Airborne photo mosaics of the array taken before and after both events helped sharpen position estimates. Radar position data helped, but the data contained position errors.

The ffFPs failed to provide significant data during *Wahoo* for several reasons. Outside the atoll, FPs were necessarily free-floating due to the cost and time required to moor them in deep water. Instead, they towed a small drogue chute to reduce their drift rate, providing better position information. Forty-eight ffFPs were placed at predetermined positions by helicopters and aircraft starting at H-2 and allowed to drift until recovered.

The Navy recovered only 10 ffFPs. This was partially due to communication failures between the task force recovery units and JTF-7 officers in charge of radiation safety, which kept them out of the recovery area for most of their allotted pickup time. In addition, a 30-minute detonation delay resulted in greater position errors for the ffFPs that were recovered. In spite of the data loss during *Wahoo*, their potential utility in augmenting the radiation field data was too great not to deploy them again in *Umbrella*.

Because *Umbrella* took place inside the atoll in shallow, calm water, data collection was much more successful and resulted in an estimated 80% data recovery success from coracles and ffFPs and 90% from target ships. None of the coracle moors failed, although seven close-in coracles overturned shortly after detonation for unknown reasons. Calculations had shown water wave, shockwave overpressure, and base surge wind forces not strong enough to capsize a coracle. Time-of-overturn comparisons with dose rate histories were inconclusive in determining a single phenomenon, such as the arrival of the base surge, to be responsible. Why so many of the close-in coracles overturned is still a mystery.

GITR data for the time before overturn were valid, and once upside down in the water, the instruments continued to work and provided valid, although attenuated, measurements of the radiation field. (More calculations for me!) There were some instrument failures aboard one of the destroyers during *Umbrella* due to battery and electrical cable wear that occurred during the *Wahoo* rearming. The ffFP data success augmented the GITR total dose records, increasing the density of records, which helped generate accurate isodose contours throughout the array.

Coracle and Film Pack Position Reconstruction

Part of my task in sorting and organizing the data from *Umbrella* for the interim report involved plotting the locations of the coracles and recovered ffFPs. This time, we efficiently employed Task Group 7.4's helicopters and Task Group 7.3's surface teams under the eye of the USS Boxer's fire-control radar to record their positions. Initial, pre-burst, and final pickup positions provided individual ffFP movement tracks during engulfment by the base surge. This task involved hours of my time plotting the initial, H-0, and final coordinates for each instrument relative to surface zero.

Figure 18 shows instrument positions in the *Umbrella* array. Comparison of figure 18 and figure 16, the planned array, shows the ffFP movement that I had to contend with during *Umbrella* data reconstruction. Luckily, low, consistent winds occurred throughout the test period. Outside the atoll, ffFP drift was considerably greater than inside due to greater current, as shown by ffFP # 210 (lowest drift track in figure 18).

Since the coracles and destroyers remained stationary, most of the position effort and assessment of drift fell on the ffFPs. Only first-order position data were prepared while on Parry for the interim report. We checked instrument positions twice to compare with the expanding base surge movement for the final report. Using instrument track and base-surge dynamics, a comparison between the GITR and ffFP data and the expected dose rates and total doses from our models was possible.

GITR and IFC Data Analysis

Cesium (137) and Cobalt (60) provided gamma sources to calibrate the GITRs before and after each event, assuring that the total dose rate error contributed as little as possible when generating isodose contours over the array. Directional response was critical to cover coracle roll angle when engulfed in the base-surge turbulence. Significant coracle position errors occurred in a few instances: an intolerable ± 200 feet in today's field experiments. In addition, base surge radioactive material distribution uniformity, coracle motion, coracle shielding, etc., all add up to produce errors in the final analysis. Error analysis would dog me the remainder of my career.

In spite of the care taken during calibration, the GITR had limitations at high dose rates. Because it averaged over rapidly changing radiation fields, measured peak dose rates could be low by an indeterminate amount. Fortunately, early time, very high dose rates were also of very short duration so that the total measured dose accumulated over the entire event was still quite accurate. Walt was an artist negotiating such data issues.

The GITOUT (GITR tape readout) consisted of a stack of electronics developed by the Nucleonics Division and our group to convert voltage pulses responding to the magnitude of the radiation field intensity into Roentgens per hour (R/hr). By today's standards, the GITOUT's three racks of off-the-shelf electronics, consisting of amplifiers, pulse-shaping electronics, discriminators, log-converters, and tape recorders, look primitive, but they worked well. Walt Gurney, GITOUT operator throughout Hardtack I, also conducted the required data analysis back at NRDL during preparation of the final report.

Fallout from the base surge on coracle and ship surfaces mixing into the near-surface water contributed to the total radiation field film packs and GITRs measured. IFC's incremental fallout collection near the GITRs provided a time history of the deposited radionuclides and an early estimate of the deposited radiation immediately after recovery operations ceased. IFC tray samples were flown back to NRDL for more careful analysis within 6 days.

Wahoo and *Umbrella* detonations produced a mix of 31 key weapon fission products and induced early time radionuclides. Their composite radiation decay time history over the first 22 days was projected back to determine the radiation level 1 minute after detonation. If only weapon fission products were present, this process could have been very accurate, and when IFC measurements taken at two different times are backed to M+1, the projected abundance of fission products should be nearly identical, except for small timing uncertainties and counting statistics. However, physical separation of radionuclides (fractionation) can cause larger errors, making these analyses difficult and imprecise.

Pure U^{235} and Pu^{239} fission products are well understood, and forensic analysis of any contaminants gives information about the origin, composition, and chemical history of the nuclear device. Fractionation for NRDL radiochemists was alteration of the normal distribution of fission products by mechanical or chemical process. An example of a mechanical process occurred in *Umbrella* when the bubble vented to the atmosphere, losing part of its gaseous radionuclide content instead of mixing it with the water forming the column and base surge. Chemical fractionation also occurred in *Umbrella* due to the introduction of bottom coral material that underwent nuclear activation.

Between the two events, we obtained 37 standard and 12 high-intensity GITR records from the coracles and ships. Data from 72 film packs, coracles, and 20 ship locations augmented the GITR records with total dose measurements (primarily from *Umbrella*). In addition, we obtained a total of 11 underwater coracle GITR records. Coracles and ships carrying IFCs provided successful data from 26 locations between the two shots.

FIGURES

Figure 1, Chapter 1. NRDL, Building 815, located on the Hunters Point Naval Shipyard (circa 1985). Display photo taken by the author during a visit to the Iron Mountain records storage facility in December 2013.

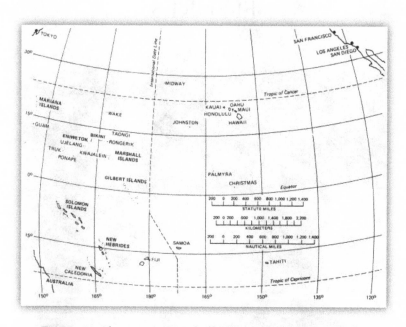

Figure 2, Chapter 2. Marshall Islands Map showing the location of Kwajalein, Enewetak, and Bikini Atolls (https://en.wikipedia.org/wiki/Pacific_Proving_Grounds, accessed 9/28/2018).

Figure 3, Chapter 2. Operations Crossroads, Shot *Able*, (yield 23 KT. /23,000 tons of TNT, equivalent), airdropped and set off 520 feet above an array of ships in Bikini Atoll on July 1, 1946 (http://www.en.wikipedia.org/wiki /Operation Crossroads, accessed 13/12/2016).

Figure 4, Chapter 2. Operation Crossroads, Shot *Baker* (yield 23 KT, Bikini Atoll, July 25, 1946), an underwater burst suspended at 90 feet, halfway between the surface and the atoll bottom (http://www.en.wikipedia.org/wiki/ Operation Crossroads, accessed 13/12/2016).

Figure 5, Chapter 2. The captured German Cruiser *Prinz Eugen* being scrubbed by sailors to reduce the radiation levels after Operation Crossroads, Shot *Baker*. Notice the lack of protective clothing and radiation-monitoring equipment (http://en.wikipedia.org/wiki/Operation_Crossroads, accessed 15/12/2016).

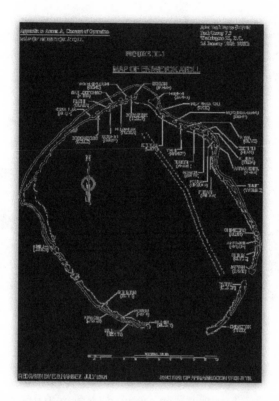

Figure 6, Chapter 4. Enewetak Atoll showing individual island names given by the Navy during World War II (in parentheses) and those used during Hardtack I (Reprinted from L.H. Berkhouse, et al., Operation Sandstone, 1948, DNA 6033F (Washington: Defense Nuclear Agency, December 19, 1983), p. 20.).

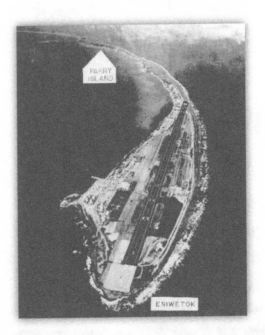

Figure 7, Chapter 4. Enewetak Island photo taken after WW II during the nuclear weapons tests showing landing strip and Parry Island in the distance (https://en.wikipedia.org/wiki/Enewetak_Atoll, accessed 18/16/2016).

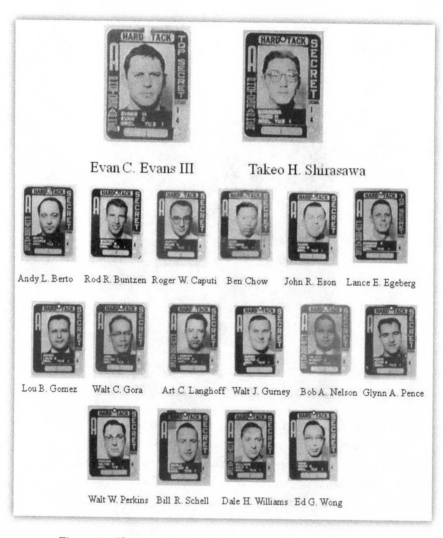

Figure 8, Chapter 4. Hardtack I security badges for NRDL Project 2.3 personnel (Author's photo collection).

Figure 9, Chapters 4, 6. Sonoma Beach Club, Ross Fuller sitting, Norm Alvarez standing left, and Bill Schell standing in the middle. The others are not identified (Author's photo collection).

Figure 10, Chapter 6. Sonoma Beach Club party showing Bill Schell being interned by Glynn Pence and Walt Gurney after he had consumed only 2–3 drinks (Bill Schell's photo collection).

Figure 11, Chapter 7 Surface event associated with Shot Wigwam, Operation Wigwam. The device was a B-7 (Mk-90, ~ 30 KT) Betty depth bomb suspended by a 2000 ft cable under a barge. (https://en.wikipedia.org/wiki/File:Wigwam, accessed 5/23/2016.)

Figure 12, Chapter 7. Shot Swordfish. Operation Domi nic, May 1962 (~10 KT, RUR-5 Antisubmarine Rocket/ASROC), detonated at 650 feet in very deep water. The AS ROC was fired from the USS *Agerholm* at a target raft 4,348 yards away. (https://commons.wikimedia.org/wiki/File:Nu celar_depth_charge_explodes_near_USS_Agerholm_(DD-826)_on_11_May_1962.jpg, accessed 7/23/2018.)

Figure 13, Chapter 7. Plume from Shot *Wahoo*, Operation Hardtack I (9 KT, at 500 feet depth, May 1958) (Glasstone, S., editor, *The Effects of Nuclear Weapons*, 1962, U.S. Government Printing Office, p. 62.

Figure 14, Chapter 7. Plume from Shot *Umbrella*, Operation Hardtack I (8 KT on bottom at 175 feet). Photo was taken from Pokon or Mui Island. During recovery operations, my instrument-recovery DUKW was located inside the atoll upwind, north of the plume (https://commons.wikimedia. org/wiki/File:Hardtack_Umbrella_nuke.jpg, accessed 5/5/206).

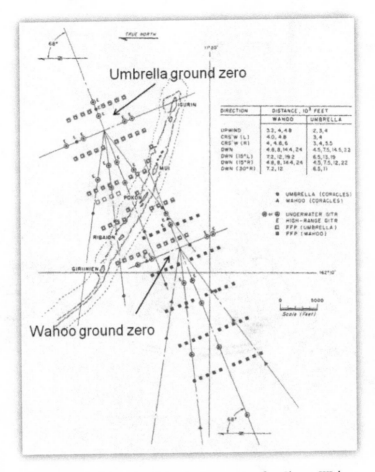

Figure 15, Chapter 7. Instrument arrays for Shots *Wahoo* and *Umbrella* used for planning purposes. Actual positions were modified closer to shot time to account for updated wind and current drift conditions (see Figure 20). Data reconstruction and analysis provided the actual instrument positions during Operation Hardtack I (Evans, E.C., and T.H. Shirasawa, *OPERATION HARDTACK, Project 2.3– Characteristics of the Radioactive Cloud from Underwater Bursts,*" Extracted version of WT-1621 (EX), DNA, AD-A995-467, 1 September 1985, Figure 1.1, p. 27).

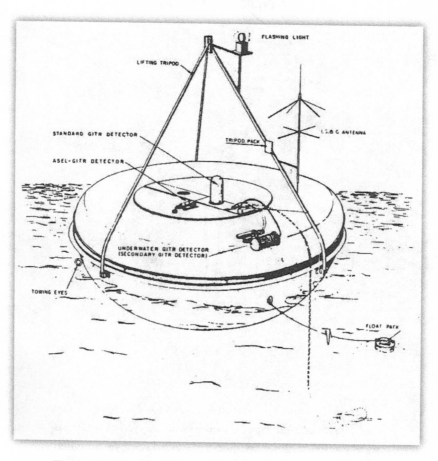

Figure 16, Chapter 7. Project 2.3 coracle containing gamma radiation field and fallout-sampling instrumentation (Evans and Shirasawa, 1985, Figure 1.2, p. 28).

Figure 17, Chapter 8. Shot *Oak*, Operation Hardtack, (8.9 MT, June 1958, surface burst) about two minutes after detonation from 20 miles away on Perry Island (http:// nuclearweaponarchive.org/Usa/Tests/Ht1oak1.jpg, accessed 1/14/2019

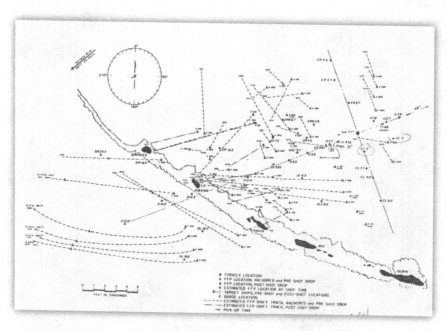

Figure 18, Chapter 9. Master plot of instrument stations and
their movement during Shot *Umbrella*, Operation Hardtack
I (Evans, E.C., and T.H. Shirasawa, 1985, Figure 2.2, p. 51).

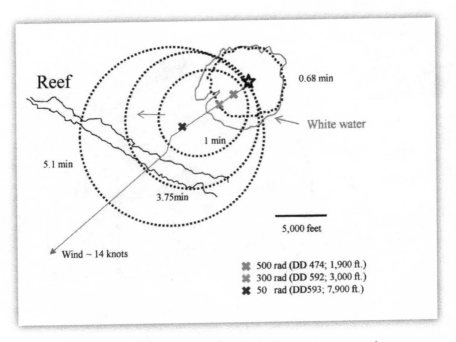

Figure 19, Chapter 9. Shot *Umbrella* base surge expansion and drift at different times. Locations of the total radiation dose due to the base surge passage are shown. **Xs** mark 500, 300, and 50 rad respectively from surface zero. White water marks radioactive patch final boundary. (Evans and Shirasawa, 1985, p. 292 for a summary of ships dose tables).

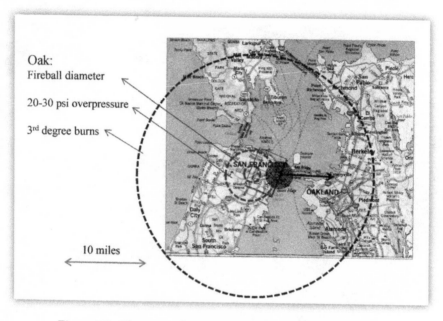

Figure 20, Chapter 9. San Francisco Bay Area map showing estimated radiological and blast hazard areas for *Umbrella* and *Oak*-like nuclear detonations. The dark circle represents the base surge from an *Umbrella*-like detonation, carried by the wind toward Oakland.

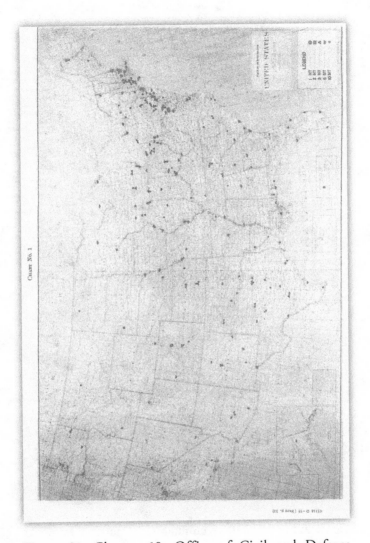

Figure 21, Chapter 10. Office of Civil and Defense Mobilization, laydown of Soviet Union nuclear warheads in an all-out attack on the U.S. ("Biological and Environmental Effects of Nuclear War," Hearings before the Special Subcommittee on Radiation, Part 1, 1959, U.S. Printing Office, Washington, Chart 1).

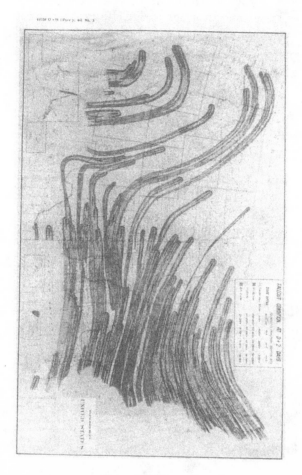

Figure 22, Chapter 10. Accumulative fallout dose estimates two days after an all-out nuclear attack by the Soviet Union ("Biological and Environmental Effects of Nuclear War," Hearings before the Special Subcommittee on Radiation, Part 1, 1959, U.S. Printing Office, Washington, Chart 4).

Figure 23, Chapter 10. Building 815 6th floor north elevator shaft showing current building interior structure (Author's photo collection).

Figure 24, Afterword. Aerial photo of the Runit Island dome covering the crater created by Shot Cactus during Operation Hardtack I. Between 1977 and 1980, the crater was used as containment for nearly 100,000 cubic meters of radioactive soil from islands in the Enewetak Atoll that was generated during the nuclear weapons tests (http://www.en.wikipedia.org/wiki/Enewetak_Atoll, accessed 9/12/2018).